Corporate Canada

Corporate Canada

14 Probes into the Workings of a Branch-Plant Economy

A Last Post Special

Edited by Rae Murphy and Mark Starowicz
With an Introduction by Mel Watkins

James Lewis & Samuel, Publishers
Toronto
1972

ISBN   0-88862-022-5 (cloth)
       0-88862-023-3 (paper)

Library of Congress Catalogue Card No. 72-90588

Design by Lynn Campbell

James Lewis & Samuel, Publishers
35 Britain Street
Toronto 229
Canada

Printed and bound in Canada

Contents

Introduction
by Mel Watkins

Where does power lie in a contemporary economy such as Canada's? From the title and subtitle onwards, this book gives a clear answer. It lies with the giant corporations. A few are Canadian-owned—as Canadian as Eaton's and the CPR. The rest are truncated Canadian portions of global giants mostly headquartered in the United States. But they all seem to have one thing in common. They are up to their armpits in the public trough, not paying taxes with one hand, grabbing subsidies with the other, and manipulating governments with both. It's what *Fortune* would call a profitable interface between business and government. It's what David Lewis, the federal leader of the New Democratic Party, calls corporate welfare bums. This book offers a series of case studies in what some readers may regard not merely as the anatomy of a branch-plant economy, but as the pathology of dependent capitalism.

If you are one of the fortunate few who has been subscribing to the *Last Post* since its inception—or who gets it the hard way by wading through the American junk in the magazine racks—you will still welcome having these journalistic essays in Canadian political economy pulled together in one handy place. It not only makes for easier reference, but a continuous reading through makes the pattern of Canadian corporate misbehaviour clearer. The rest of you are about to be exposed to some of the best popular writing being done in this country today.

Notwithstanding the obvious fact that a branch-plant economy has a limited need for highly trained and creative people, increasing numbers of Canadians are going to community colleges and universities. In the process, a considerable portion are being exposed to courses in economics and political science. If you are in that category, buy this book, for it is a useful antidote to the essential irrelevance of what mostly goes on in the classroom and the conventional textbooks.

Today, in the last half of the twentieth century AD, it is possible to study economics and political science and remain completely uninformed about where power lies. Indeed, if my own university is typical, it is not only possible but highly probable.

The conventional economist, entrapped by the long shadow of Adam Smith, whom he has typically not read (and therefore blissfully unaware of the master's subtleties), believes two things about power. The first is that it is diffused through the market. Models of price determination under monopoly and oligopoly (a few sellers with market power) he can discuss at length, but his basic faith remains unshaken. Otherwise he risks discovering political economy and finding most of his present skills obsolete. The second is that the state is potentially omnipotent and benevolent, a neutral entity able to intervene when the populace wills to correct any imbalance. Believe that, and you will never risk discovering *political* economy and understanding the reality of the capitalist state.

The political scientist, at least the Canadian variant thereof, carries around a good deal less theoretical baggage than the economist, but typically serves us no better. In the nature of the case, his primary concern is the state and its structures but, liberal ideologue that he is, the state is the pluralistic state that mediates among competing interest groups. The result is a built-in bias which leads to more attention being focused on the Senate than on General Motors.

Ideas shade off into ideologies and ideologies into propaganda and lies. The process of mystification begun in the academies trickles downwards into the media. The cavorting of politicians is hard news; the activities of corporations are buried in the "business section," antiseptically reported and fondly analysed. In any event, the corporation can hedge its bets with splashy advertisements accompanied by an unwritten right to censor what's sandwiched in between.

No more striking example of the effectiveness of these techniques is to be found than in the regular reports of opinion pollsters that the public regards big unions as more of a threat to them than big business—and ranks big government as the number two enemy. But what else is to be expected when a union settlement of a 16 per cent wage increase over two years merits a headline on page one and a whining editorial denouncing it, while an increase in corporate profits of 32 per cent is buried in a two-paragraph story on page twenty-eight and hailed by the financial columnists as evidence of a business recovery.

Liberalism has long had a tight grip in North America but never a total monopoly. There has always been some dissent to preserve our sanity, and recently it has been growing. As a mode of thinking and analysis, Marxism has survived at the intellectual periphery, and whatever its tendency to be vulgarized for sectarian purposes, it offers a clearly superior answer to liberalism on the question of where power lies. Contemporary Marxists see the giant corporation as the central institution of capitalism in its highest and imperialist phase. Since the great merger movement and cartelization of the late nineteenth century, competitive capitalism has given way to monopoly capitalism, and the corporation as capitalist has achieved market power not only through its ability to set prices, but more fundamentally through its ability to appropriate and allocate surplus by the ploughing back of earnings and superior access to finance capital, and to manipulate tastes and sustain demand through the sales effort.

Marx himself offered a penetrating insight into the nature of the capitalist state which is difficult to improve upon in his famous observation: "The executive of the modern state is but a committee for managing the common affairs of the whole bourgeoisie." In hinterland areas, it is the owners, top managers and financiers of the foreign-based multinational corporations that are the contemporary ruling class. Where power lies is mostly outside of Canada. (Hence a nationalism of the left is a legitimate means of transcending alienation and powerlessness.)

As a social democratic or left-liberal academic, Pierre Trudeau could relate, up to a point, to the desire of Canadians for more economic independence—as the last essay in this book reminds us. But as leader of the Liberal Party and prime minister, he has learned from whence campaign funds come and where power lies. When Senator Stanbury tells us that ninety-five corporations bankroll the Liberal Party, you and I know the odds are that two out of three of them are foreign-controlled, and four out of five of those two-thirds American-controlled. The Trudeau government having already gutted tax reform and anti-monopoly legislation under pressure from the business community, we are not surprised when it emasculates even the modest proposals of the Gray report on foreign ownership. Appointing Mr. Gray, a junior minister from a Windsor constituency, to deal with this delicate problem was not exactly taking risks, as the essay in this book on Ford, also as it happens of Windsor, makes clear. Perhaps you expected more from Mr. Trudeau after he got that self-proclaimed go-ahead for independence from Mr. Nixon last December? But that's not the only message he may be presumed to have got. "Mr. Trudeau left for Washington at 1 p.m. on Monday and arrived back in Ottawa at 1 p.m. yesterday. He met with President Nixon for more than two hours Monday afternoon and later the two men continued their talks at a 'working dinner' at the White House. Among the 35 guests at the dinner were Edward Cole, president of General Motors Corp., and B. R. Dorsey, president of Gulf Oil Co." You didn't read that in Canadian newspapers, but you could have in the *Wall Street Journal* of December 8, 1971.

In the media, dissent has tended to be marginal in the extreme and to take the form of muckraking. As befits a colonized country, Canada's greatest practicing muckraker was the American Gustavus Myers, and it is one of the happy coincidences of our times that his classic *History of Canadian Wealth*, Vol. I, has just been reprinted, and by James Lewis & Samuel. No volume two has ever been found, for the good reason that it was apparently never written. This book is the best substitute going, with the additional merit that, being authored by Canadians, it shows an indigenous capacity to rake muck that promises ill for the corporations and their political flunkies.

My purpose in this preface has been to suggest that pieces written under the pressure of a magazine deadline have stood the test of time and merit the longevity and wider readership that this book will give them. As a university teacher, I welcome an addition to the still too-short list of books that are increasingly enabling those of us who wish to cease teaching the conventional wisdom of economics and political science in separate compartments, to begin to teach the political economy of Canada. As a socialist, I welcome these exposés of the corporation and the state, for the subversion of these institutions is a necessary, though hardly a sufficient condition for moving towards a better world.

If the reader has borne with me this far, he—or she, since you, unlike academics, tend to come in both sexes—is entitled to move on to the main course. Permit me only a final and more personal note. I like most in this book the opening piece on Eaton's. For one thing, it would be indeed to miss the main chance if, in our new and proper concern about foreign capitalists in Canada, we failed to appreciate the seamier side of our own indigenous beast. But the essay also brings remembrances of things past. As a boy in rural Ontario, where paper was scarce, Eaton's catalogue filled a multiplicity of purposes, finally to be recycled in the outdoor privy. One should have sensed then that anything so slick and glossy to the feel couldn't be all good.

Foreword

When the first issue of the *Last Post* came off the press in Montreal in December of 1969, the stirrings of a new era in Canadian politics were apparent. Nationalist feeling was rising, and major political realignments were taking place. Two themes predominated, and remain today the pivots of political debate in this country: Quebec, and Canada's position as a cultural and economic satellite of the United States. As a new political journal in a period when people began to thirst for fresh information, the *Last Post* naturally devoted most of its pages throughout that period to those two themes.

This book is a selection of the major articles carried by the *Last Post* on the Canadian economy since the magazine appeared. (A companion volume, *Quebec: A Chronicle 1968-1972*, contains the major pieces on the recent turbulent years in Quebec.) Although the articles were written by different authors at different times, the focus of the nationalist debate has lent a unity and continuity to the pieces in this book.

The articles have been revised to eliminate awkward time references, repetition and errors. In some cases, such as the account of Joe Greene's blunders in the continental energy debacle of 1970, we have let the piece stand as a historical account; to follow the intricate vagaries of the energy question up to date would require an entire book in itself.

We hope that *Corporate Canada* will serve as a layman's guide to the basics of Canada's economic and political crisis. And while it is certainly no economics text, it should serve the student well in a field where current economic writing is often as irrelevant as it is moribund.

Although he doesn't appear in our list of contributors at the end of the book, honourable mention is due Drummond Burgess, the managing editor of the *Last Post*, who first edited this material and guided it to publication in the magazine. And the *Last Post* is not only its editors and writers, but the many journalists, trade unionists, researchers, academics and anonymous allies in the cobwebs of the government and civil service, who not only agreed that a new kind of journalism was needed in Canada, but saw that it was possible and worked to achieve it.

Rae Murphy
Mark Starowicz

Part One
Waking Up from the National Dream

In the sudden flurry of concern over foreign domination of the Canadian economy, too little attention has been paid to the important sectors of the economy that are still in Canadian hands, or to the intrepid survivors of a once-powerful indigenous capitalist elite. We now have the beginnings, at least, of a body of literature examining the role of multinational corporations and the politics of continental trade. But examinations of our native business institutions are scarce, and are normally left to the uncritical pages of the business press or to the wintry heights of economic journals. A thesis of this book is that the failure to develop an independent economy can be laid on the doorsteps of Canadian business and government as much as on those of the American multinationals; for that reason, we begin with a section on Canadian 'institutions'. Through a portrait of the quaint Eaton's empire, a pocket history of the CPR and an examination of the dying Canadian farm, we trace some of the perils of the idea that the national interest has been served by turning over control of the economy to the logic of corporate interests.

There has been a tendency, perceptible in what we can loosely call the growing 'nationalist movement', to take a charitable approach to Canadian corporations, presumably because survival merits kindness. Some, of course, would prefer a Canadian conglomerate to an American conglomerate; that's a sentiment current these days in some schools of thought—in what we characterize, for example, as Maclean's-Magazine Nationalism (Fourteen-Canadian-Millionaires-and-How-They-Got-That-Way sort of thing). It is our opinion that how they got that way often merits contempt as much as how an American got that way. And that is why the first chapter of this section, and of the book, deals with what is probably the most Canadian business institution of them all—Eaton's.

Eaton's is a conglomerate in every sense of the word. It bought out small stovemakers, furniture manufacturers, shirtmakers and the like by becoming their major customer. Once that small entrepreneur depended on Eaton's for eighty per cent of his business, it was a small step to buy him out or just turn him into a branch operation. Thus were born the many Eaton brands in manufactured goods.

Eaton's is, in a way, a microcosm of what has happened to Canadian business—the smaller manufacturer becoming dependent on the big customer, the customer in the latter case being the United States. And the analogy can be extended to how Eaton's became so powerful that it could order local governments around.

The history of Eaton's teaches us another important lesson—that the decline of the smaller Canadian manufacturer is due not only to external pressure, but also to internal economic policy that has fostered conglomerates like Eaton's.

Above all, it was our intention when we began the project to compile the first and only counter-history of Eaton's, to inject some scepticism into the nationalist debate and cast some doubt on the wisdom of laying down the flower of our youth to defend the hegemony of some of the most unpresentable people in our history.

For, after all, the Eatons themselves were stridently nationalist (in an Empire sort of way). When there were rumours that the firm might sell to an American concern, the founder's son looked down his nose and said, "There is not sufficient money in the world to buy my father's name." Now there may be those who take some satisfaction from watching our own home-grown arrivistes pouring contempt on the heads of the undeniably crasser and even-more-recently arrived American variety. But in facing the threat of the US real-estate developer, we would suggest, a return to Jalna should not be the beacon to guide us.

Similarly, a glance at the history and current policy of a key national asset, the CPR, leaves little cause to inspire the Canadian nationalist.

Oddly, it was Jean Marchand who put the matter in correct perspective: "Transportation policy," he said, "is closely tied to economic planning and as such must be linked to the common good and not the profitability of private enterprise."

The chapter on "Why the CPR Doesn't Like You" suggests that the common good has not been the chief concern of the men who run the CPR. It is precisely this kind of yielding of national priorities to the exigencies of private interests that has led, quite logically, to a weak and easily co-optable economy.

At the other end of the scale, there are the small Canadian manufacturers, store owners, independent fishermen and farmers. Little attention is paid them in the current concerns over foreign domination because we tend to think of the problem as being industrial, and therefore purely eastern-urban.

But the challenge from the domestic and international corporation has had a profound impact on these people. The third chapter in this section focuses on one group among them and traces the way in which the conglomerate and the multinational have eroded the basis of an entire sector of the Canadian economy, and begun to displace a whole class. The price of a government policy that allows the economy to drift in the currents of the continental market can be seen most concretely in the lingering death of the Canadian farm, in the decline of a way of life and the steady exodus of men and women from regions of the country that have been declared "economically irrelevant" to the priorities of the planners.

Eaton's: An Irreverent History
by Mark Starowicz

Timothy comes to the Big Town

Early to bed
Early to rise
Never get tight
And — ADVERTISE.

— Methodist preacher's slogan

It's doubtful that even an Eaton's publication today would write of Timothy Eaton the way a company history wrote of the founder in 1919:

"He reminds one of Cromwell smashing into the effete Parliament of Charles I; or of Cecil Rhodes founding a commonwealth among savages."

The Cecil Rhodes and the savages part would have application to the attitudes of some of his later heirs, but Timothy was a rather straightforward, even dour Presbyterian-turned-Methodist who arrived in Toronto in 1869 with $6500 and settled down to the business of making money.

He paid the $6500 for Jenning's dry-goods business on Yonge Street and embarked on what was, to his just credit, a revolution in Canadian retailing.

The money he brought with him came from seven years' partnership in a store with his older brother in St. Mary's, near Stratford. Timothy had always earned his money by hard labour in the best Presbyterian tradition.

Since he had gone through a hard, seven-year apprenticeship in a store in Ulster before he emigrated to Canada, he had an appreciation of what it meant to work hard for a trying employer. As a result, he was to be an understanding, if strict employer himself, concerned about his staff's welfare.

He would lead the country in introducing shorter working hours for his staff, and paid welfare and pensions before

*Published in the *Last Post*, February 1970.

most employers had heard of those terms. But he could not abide labour unions when they arose towards the latter part of his life—that interfered with the intense paternalism and strict authority with which he ran his store. That much, his heirs learned from him.

The retail revolution Timothy Eaton launched in Canada was based on two tenets:

Cash only; instead of the credit and running charge system that most retail stores in Canada then worked on; and

One price only, which wiped out the dickering over prices that was the accepted shopping method in Canada.

Later, "satisfaction guaranteed or money returned" was to be a slogan that shook some of Eaton's competitors. Then Timothy learned the values of advertising, and that became another ingredient of the rise of the Eaton empire: constant, saturation advertising.

His rural ingenuity extended to paying the horse-drawn streetcar drivers to cry out "Everybody out for Eaton's" when they pulled up before the store—a modern day equivalent being the curious way Eaton's has direct access to the Toronto and Montreal subways, so that a large part of the passenger traffic can't get out without walking through the stores.

But the major revolution was the Eaton's catalogue. In a fragmented country where vast numbers of people had no access to modern products, this was the only way to shop. In the early years of this century, the Eaton's catalogue was an integral part of the culture, an indispensable text that was used not only to shop, but also to learn English.

When Timothy died in 1907, the massive Winnipeg branch had been opened; mail order was a separate unit and the firm had its own buying offices throughout the world and employed 9,000 people. He left his heirs a personal fortune estimated at anywhere from $3,000,000 to $15,000,000. Sales that year totalled over $22,000,000.

Jack Eaton, later to become Sir John Eaton, an unreconstructed reactionary, took over the firm. He and his wife Flora became the unofficial First Family of Canada—patrons of the arts, builders of the stately family pleasure-dome, Ardwold, owners of yachts, villas, private railroad cars, horse stables.

Under Jack Eaton, and later Robert Y. Eaton and John

David Eaton, the empire grew to become the third largest employer in Canada, after the federal government and the railroads. Its 50,000 year-round employees are supplemented by 15,000 part-time workers over Christmas. The Eaton family is the sole owner of forty-eight department stores across Canada, five warehouses and service buildings, factories, 352 catalogue sales offices, large tracts of strategic downtown land and the personal Eaton estates and fortune. The tag on the Eaton empire is estimated at $400,000,000. When John David's home in Toronto was robbed a few years ago, the jewels stolen were valued at $1,000,000.

The Eaton empire is more than that.

It is one of the most powerful concentrations of wealth, economic power and political influence in Canada, ranking with E. P. Taylor's Argus Corporation, the Canadian Pacific Railway and Power Corporation. It is also an empire that wields this imposing power whenever something stands in its way.

It is a structure whose history and methods reveal much about the country itself, and the financial and political elite that ran it through Eaton's boom years. It is a firm that has cowed newspapers into silence, ordered municipal governments around and maintained a large reservoir of political influence to this day.

While propagating the mythology that it was only interested in serving the interests of the country and its people, it wrote a history of reaction, manipulation and entrenchment, erecting a tower of wealth on a mountain of low salaries, poor working conditions and arbitrary management. Yet in certain periods it led in pensions, shorter hours and welfare benefits to employees, and in the play of these seeming contradictions it erected an institution that has had a profound effect on Canadian life, and reflected much of this country's history—not all of it laudable.

It begs examination, because that is precisely what it has always successfully stifled.

All that glitters

How ya gonna keep' em down on the farm
After they've seen Paree?
— Post-war song

After the sweet came the dessert of fruit and it was at this luncheon that I learned, from the example of the Duchess and the Princess, how to eat a fine ripe peach with a spoon. They used a knife to cut the fruit open, removed the pit with knife and fork, and then picked up the dessert spoon and ate the two halves from the skin, in the same way as melon is eaten. This is now one of my mealtime habits, and one doesn't have the messy business of peeling the fruit.
— *from the memoirs of Lady Eaton*

Canadians have always been a straightforward folk, aware of their place in the order of things and not given to assuming postures patently beyond their class standing. The British were always more cultured and commanding, the Americans smarter and richer—the Canadians were, as the French say, "Nés pour un petit pain."

Nothing was more revealing of our secret longing to scrape the dung off our boots, however, than that curious period when Canada tried to produce its own aristocracy, heaped adulation on Lady Eaton as Mrs. Canada, and sent her on a tour of every Rotary Club west of Yonge Street. And we have very few more revealing glimpses into the nature of that Canadian ruling class she symbolized, the principles and ethics they espoused, the social system they sought to erect (successfully for a while), before they gently gave their seats away to the pleasant young men from New York with the blueprints.

Flora McCrea, born in Omemee, Ontario, married John Craig Eaton in 1901, and from the twenties onward became the matriarch of the family—"A great traveller and social leader ... a staunch patron of the arts ..." hails the official Eaton's history.

In 1915, when John Craig Eaton, president of the firm until his death in 1922, was knighted for his service to the war (he paid for a machine-gun battery), she became Lady Eaton.

In her autobiography, entitled *Memory's Wall* and published in 1956, Lady Eaton coyly pretended to be writing only to her clan, so that "you will be enabled to know me better," but allowed the public to peek into the lives and times of this vice-regal family. One of the undiscovered gems of Canadian literature, *Memory's Wall* is an exercise in name-dropping, in

Mark Starowicz / 9

recalling all the great parties that were held and who attended them wearing what, a literary rattling of jewels that borders on the arriviste. Here is a home-grown empress dowager mooning publicly over the loyalty of servants, over the lovely people of the Toronto elite, recalling with thrills the times she was presented to the Court in Buckingham Palace, and allowing the unwashed to derive inspiration and pride by peeking in on these idyllic moments.

The attitudes of this matriarch from Omemee also reflect the ideas of the Eaton family and their concept of divine mission, and bring us closer to understanding the roots and nature of the paternalism that is the bedrock of the Eaton empire.

In a diary Lady Eaton wrote on a Maritimes fishing trip, which she published privately for distribution to her friends, she made these observations on the Quebec conscription crisis of 1917:

"We went on past the new park overlooking the River Valley and around the Plains of Abraham, and back through the New St. Louis Gate to the Chateau. We had dinner and afterwards walked up and down the Dufferin terrace where so many have walked through many years—where so much of the history of Canada has been cradled; and now in another crisis of our country we walk amidst it, our own countrymen speaking a foreign tongue; through misunderstanding and ignorance evading the responsibilities of the country whose advantages they enjoy; and one wonders what eventually will be the outcome. They are sheep without a shepherd, without even a sheep dog to keep them straight; but they are a simple-living people, and we cannot help feeling that if the present question of conscription is handled with care and explained to them (for it is largely that they do not understand it) then there will be no trouble." *(Rippling Rivers,* September 1917.)

The Eatons at that time owned a private railroad car, a yacht, palatial mansions and a villa in Florence. Lady Eaton frequently travelled to Italy to get away from it all, and fondly recalled her travels in her book. But she omitted some of her more interesting impressions of that happy land; fortunately, they were recorded by the *Toronto Daily Star,* October 19, 1927:

ITALY NOW HAPPIEST LAND
SAYS LADY EATON RETURNING
PRAISES MUSSOLINI'S RULE

FOUND WHOLE COUNTRY IMPROVED, PEOPLE
    HAPPIEST IN WORLD —
ADMIRES SIGNORA MUSSOLINI FOR HER
    DOMESTIC QUALITIES —
EUROPEAN COUNTRIES UNPROGRESSIVE IN
    CARING FOR SICK

In the article she is quoted as saying how nice it was that "no more do the beggars in the streets and around the cathedrals annoy everyone" and laments that "Mussolini is not really in good health, he suffers intense pain and the only relief he gets is in distracting his thoughts by playing his violin."

She also pronounced herself on womanhood:

" 'I may be called antiquated for some of my ideas,' Lady Eaton said, 'For I am not one of these "votes for women" women. I do not see that women have gained much by the vote—it has merely complicated the problem because the vote is not restricted to intelligent women. I think the vote is rather a nuisance myself.'

"Lady Eaton considers that a woman can find no greater sphere of endeavour than in her own home. 'I may sound old-fashioned in saying that,' Lady Eaton said, 'but I believe that women have lost sight of that fact to a certain extent and that they are coming back to it.' "

On November 16 she sang at Massey Hall for Toronto's elite, and the *Toronto Star* burbled:

VOICE OF RARE SWEETNESS
CHARMS TORONTO AUDIENCE

The flavour of the fawning review is not to be missed:

"Luigi Von Kunitz tapped with his baton on his desk. The orchestra paused from its overture. A slender figure came from under the curtained archway and advanced quickly through the maze of chairs and music stands. The conductor left his platform to meet her and escort her to the footlights . . . The artiste . . . bowed to left and right gracefully but not lingeringly . . . Her deep-toned 'Helas,' with which she began the aria's change from interrogation to regret, was a true cri de coeur."

Recalling her preparations for Court presentation, Lady Eaton left us this account of London manners:

"We had taken instructions in the Court curtsy from Miss Violet Vanbrugh, one of London's well-known actresses, and she had been an excellent teacher. She would say, 'Walk up to me,' then, after making us sink back on the supporting foot, she would order us to do it again, 'and remember the earth will hold you up, and don't be afraid to step up firmly.' It was important that we lift our heads after the moment of the full drop of the curtsy ... There was some difference of opinion in London about the matter of lifting one's face and smiling when presented to one's sovereign, but Miss Vanbrugh insisted on it ... How Their Majesties managed to retain their gracious composure during an evening of eight hundred presentations was a mystery, but also a lesson for the rest of us."

On one of her visits to the Winnipeg store, she made "a morning tour" of the mail-order buildings with Eaton's chief in that city, H.M. Tucker. Here she recounts how she gave the unfortunate Mr. Tucker a lesson in employee relations: "When we returned to his office, I looked at him and said, 'Mr. Tucker, that was just useless.' He asked what I meant. 'Well,' I said, 'our people were looking for some friendly contact with us, and neither of us gave it to them. Neither one of us smiled.' His reply was, 'But I don't smile readily.' And to that, I said, 'You'll have to learn, and we're both going to do better this afternoon.' After lunch we continued our tour, going this time through the Store, and I'm glad to record that Mr. Tucker smiled and I smiled too. I'm positive our afternoon's activities netted infinitely better results than the morning's."

The temptation to quote more of Lady Eaton's gems of managerial wisdom and passing observations on the problems of wealth and station is hard to resist, but suffice it to point out that her memoirs are available from any public library in this country and come highly recommended.

Thus for more than twenty years, the newspapers glittered with mentions of Lady Eaton, with descriptions of her residences, of her charitable donations, of the gala events she attended. John Craig Eaton was Sir John, and with Lady Eaton they were 'Canada's first family'. They were met by flocks of reporters when they disembarked from the luxury liners after their sojourns abroad. Lady Eaton's pronouncements on the passing scene were dutifully recorded, her attire and grace spread over the social pages of the Toronto and Montreal papers. And though Jack Eaton was a more hard-headed sort who shied away from this sort of publicity, Lady Eaton played her role well.

Here was an Edwardian Canada, a native merchant family that sought the splendour and status of a colonial aristocracy. Here was the highest ornamental development of an indigenous capitalist elite.

"The beggars around the cathedral"

Excerpts from testimony by Eaton's factory employees before the Royal Commission on Price Spreads, 1935

By Mr. Bullen (Lawyer, ILGWU)

Miss Nolan:

Q. Miss Nolan, were you employed by the T. Eaton Company, Limited, of Toronto?

A. Yes, I was . . .

Q. And when you first went there what was your basis of pay?

A. $11 was guaranteed (per 44-hour week on piecework).

Q. And after that did it ever change?

A. Yes, I got $12.50. Towards the end of 1928, it was raised to $12.50.

Q. And what was the result, first of all, physically, from this drop in rates? (Piecework rate of $3.60 for making a dozen voile dresses, which was dropped in 1933 to $1.75 a dozen for same dresses and same work.]

A. Well, you had to work so hard, you were driven so fast that, it just became impossible to make $12.50, and you were a nervous wreck. The girls cried. I was hysterical myself. It almost drove me insane.

Q. Was that condition general or did it only happen to you?

A. It was general. All the girls were the same.

Q. And did you break down by reason of it all?

A. Yes, I went into hysterics several times and I had to go

Mark Starowicz / 13

to the hospital and the nurse said, "What is the matter? You girls are always coming here."

Mrs. Annie S. Wells:

Q. You were going to tell the Committee about the material. You said it was inferior. In what way?

A. The cotton goods were full of starch—we called it starch. You know, they fill it with something to make it appear thick and strong. The manufacturer did; we did not, and of course when you turned the dress you were just smothered in starch, and the particular fault of that starch was that it raised sores on your arms.

Q. Did it hurt your breathing at all?

A. Sure. It made your throat sore and your nose stuffed up and you felt a wreck. That was easy.

Q. Was that a very prevalent condition?

A. Yes, very prevalent.

Mrs. Wells continuing:

Q. Would you mind indicating to the Commission from your standpoint as a worker why you disputed the pay for this dress? Please describe the dress, what you got per dozen for making it, and why you objected to that price?

A. Well, this dress was a cotton crepe, and we had to make the blouse with double fronts, and a frill in between on the one side. It had a raglan sleeve. That is a sleeve that is not set in; it came up to the neck here. We had to make the skirt, which consisted of three straight lengths in the front, and two pleats let in, and this had to be stitched down on the outside and finished off with a little stitching. That was that. I forget now whether the back had a pleat in it or not; I think it had one; anyway, we had to make that skirt, and then we had to join it to the blouse, and we had to sew that bow that is on the shoulder but sewn in such a position that the bow could be threaded through a button-hole. It had to be put into the right side. It was not just the trimming. Then we had to make the belt loops.

Q. How many?

A. Two belt loops and put them on the waistline for the belt to thread through. And you got $1.15 a dozen.

Q. How much?

A. $1.15 for that amount of work.

By *Mr. Sommerville: (Member of Committee)*

Q. That is about 9½ cents for a dozen of these dresses?

A. For that amount of work.

Q. You get 9½ cents for doing what you have described?

A. 9½ cents.

> *By Hon. Mr. Stevens: (Member of Committee)*

Q. What does the dress sell for?

A. The selling price is $1.59 each. It is marked here. [Later] . . . It took an ordinary four and a half to five hours to make a dozen.

Miss Amy Tucker:

Q. It has been stated here that Eaton's do countenance and recognize Unions. Have you anything to say about that?

A. When we tried to organize, Mr. Clendining said "You girls can join a Union if you please but that does not mean to say that this firm will recognize a Union. This firm will not recognize a Union."

Q. Who told you that?

A. Mr. Clendining.

Q. Anything else?

A. And then he went on to say "Of course we recognize Unions." And I said "You do in the printing, because it happens to be government work and it must have the Union label on it. But otherwise you do not recognize Unions." And in all our talk he would try to bring in racial questions, about the Jewish people, telling us we should not belong to the Union at all that was controlled by Jews.

In 1934, a remarkable figure in Canadian politics took aim at the big companies in Canada and went on a private radio and pamphlet campaign to expose the conditions of workers in factories, and the transgressions of high finance. He was all the more remarkable because he was the minister of Trade and Commerce in the Conservative government of R.B. Bennett. This man, Henry Herbert Stevens, hurt the Bennett government so much with his attacks that he was persuaded to resign in October of that same year.

But he had managed to leave a legacy—part of which was the Stevens Committee on Price Spreads, as swashbuckling a one-man attack on private interest and its role in the Depression as has ever rolled over Bay Street. The favourite target of this curious Red Tory was the retail trade. And that meant Eaton's. For the first time in history, with batteries of company lawyers kicking and screaming, the untouchable company was forced to bare its dealings, wages, capital, profits and losses.

As the Eaton dress-factory workers in Ontario were brought to testify about working conditions, salaries and battles between the International Ladies' Garment Workers Union (ILGWU) and Eaton's, a picture emerged of the sweat that was at the base of the glitter of Ardwold, the Florence villa, the Court receptions and the ecclesiastical silence of the press.

The witnesses before the committee (it was made a full royal commission in the fall of 1934) admitted that working conditions were not among the worst until the death of Sir John Eaton, and the onset of the Depression. But they made it clear where Eaton's transferred the misery that arose from the lower sales of the Depression period.

The minimum wage in Ontario at the time was $12.50 for a 44-hour week. More precisely, the law required only that 80 per cent of a department average $12.50, and the other 20 per cent were uncovered. The companies, therefore, could and did play the averages game with employees' salaries.

When the slump in buying came, its implications were immediately dumped on the factory employees. Where a dressmaker would earn $3.60 a dozen for her work on a particular voile dress, in 1933 her rate of earning was knocked down to $1.75 for the same dress, and the same work. For an eight-hour day she would, if she worked very hard, take home $2.50. Even in the Depression, this bordered on the outrageous. Eaton's de facto policy at the time was so petty that if a woman earned 33¾ cents on a piece, she did not receive the fraction but was computed at 33 cents.

With styles becoming more complicated and the dresses harder to make, the rates were not raised but drastically lowered and the women were expected to produce more, not less. Witnesses spoke of being "badgered and harassed," and "threatened if you did not make the $12.50 you would be fired." They were clocked by stop watches, disciplined for slow work by being sent home to sit out a week with no wages. If they came five minutes late for work, they were frequently locked out of the plant and forced to go home without earning anything that day.

One case out of many was that of Miss Winnifred Wells, an eighteen-year Eaton's veteran, who recounted to the commission how she was approached by one of the managers, a Mr. Jeffries, and asked if she had made her minimum for the previous Friday.

". . . I said 'No, I have not.' I think I was about 30 or 75 cents short."

The manager returned in a half hour and told her "You go home; go home and don't come back until I send for you, and we will send for you when we are ready."

She went to Jeffries' superior, a man named Conroy.

"And he said that was a new system that we are bringing in, every time a girl fell down on her work she would get a week's holiday, go home for a week.

"And I asked him if he thought that was quite fair; that was the first day in the week; I had the rest of the week to make up the $12.50. And he did not seem to consider that was anything at all . . .

". . . So I asked him how he thought a girl was going to live if she was going to be sent home every time she fell down on her money. He said it did not matter to him, none of his business, and got very angry over it."

Of course if Miss Wells were starving, she could have reported to the welfare office at Eaton's. It was a matter of company pride that it had a generous welfare office. It is in the nature of this sort of corporate paternalism to take care of the needy—and also to make sure that the welfare office is never underpopulated. Eaton's took care of its sick and destitute. But why would it never translate the funds available for welfare into a decent wage?

If the workers received a decent wage, they might get notions of having *earned* it, instead of having *received* it. And when that sort of system entered, it would threaten the existence of Ardwold. It might lead to such violations of 'family' corporatism as unions . . .

In 1934, an incident occurred that clarified Eaton's attitude towards unions.

In March and April of that year, the women of one department organized into a local of the International Ladies' Garment Workers Union. Witnesses before the commission testified that they had been warned against organizing into a union. A manager named Clendining said to the girls that they didn't need a union and told one "how would she like to go home with $6 a week and he said some of the fellows in his office went home with $6 a week; and she told him he ought to be ashamed to say that they got that . . . He told us we were out of our class, that we were mixing with the people on Spadina." (Union officials—Spadina Road is Toronto's dressmaking district.)

But the women—thirty-eight in that section—joined the union and began to ask for higher rates on some of the dresses they were working on. Eaton's made short work of them.

On July 11, after several days of asking for higher rates on a specific dress, the committee representing the women went to see management (a Mr. Moore and Clendining) to ask again if they would raise the rate, and were told definitely not—"take it or leave it." So the women stopped work that afternoon and waited to see what would happen. They were summoned to see Moore and Clendining.

". . . and Mr. Clendining asked each of us how long we had worked there. We told him. He wrote that down. Then he said 'Are you willing to work on this style?' We said no, we would like to have the price raised. He said 'Well, you can wait until 5:30. If you cannot make up your mind to work then, we no longer require you.' "

The women asked for passes out of the building to see their union officials, and were granted them. The officials urged them to go back to work and press for the higher rate without a work stoppage.

"We went back the next morning ready to work . . . We went back and the time keeper would not let us pass . . . We went up to the 9th floor. We were ready to go downstairs to take our machines and he told us our cards were out . . . We were locked out. We did not strike, we were locked out."

After 5:30 no one could get into the factory building—it was cleared by then. The women could not have been logically expected to turn up at 5:30 to announce their intention to return to work. With surgical efficiency, Eaton's had divested itself of a union group.

One of the more astonishing distortions in the official history of Eaton's—*The Store that Timothy Built* by William Stephenson—deals with the very critical and revealing series of hearings by the Stevens committee.

This is how the book writes off the damaging testimony:

"In June, 1934, to take their minds off unemployment and the breadlines, Canadians were treated to a circus staged by the federal government."

Included in the charges the firm was eventually asked to answer were:

That Eaton's practice of featuring 'loss leaders' could wreck the market for any smaller retailer dealing mainly in that commodity;

That Eaton's system of selling 'distress goods' created havoc among smaller retailers;

That Eaton's received special discounts from manufacturers for larger orders, so that it could sell these products at far below most of their competitors' prices;

That Eaton's put pressure on suppliers not to sell to others at such discounts;

That Eaton's mail-order department took everything out and put nothing back into areas where it flourished;

That the only reason Eaton's could afford to sell at such low prices even with such dubious tactics was because the firm paid very low wages and forced factory workers to toil at "intolerable speeds."

The book claims Eaton's had "no trouble" refuting these claims and that "all the other headline-making claims of 'unfair competition' and 'slave labour' were refuted with similar ease."

The ease with which Eaton's refuted these charges is, to anyone who leafs through the hundreds of pages of testimony, somewhat dubious. A reading of the report leaves no doubt that Eaton's was raked over the coals and run over by a steamroller.

The book continues to portray an utterly shaken R.Y. Eaton (then president), his feelings hurt by the investigation. It reads: ". . . R.Y. chose to view the whole inquiry as a warning that for a firm like Eaton's—the nation's storekeeper, willing servant and watchdog of excellence—profit must be considered, for lack of better word, as *sinful*, and must never be allowed to become the sole criterion of success. Never again must there be even the flimsiest excuse for an investigation."

This magnanimity obviously failed—despite the best efforts

of the firm, of course—because it is widely estimated that Eaton's is worth $400,000,000 today. Nice try, though, R.Y.

But as if the poor Eatons weren't hurt enough by the scurrilous allegations of women earning $12.50 a week, Stephenson notes in his book that "... the Stevens Committee was to make R.Y. even more conservative than he had been before."

He writes: "An even more notable manifestation of this ultra-conservatism occurred in September, 1934, when a *Telegram* reporter, in his description of the Labour Day Parade, noted that several union marchers 'dipped their flags in sorrow as they passed Eaton's.'

"R.Y. demanded a retraction. The editor replied politely that he had checked the story and found it to be true, so there was no need for a retraction."

The picture of the poor, distraught man, wounded to the quick by the Stevens committee, running around trying to censor newspapers, coupled with the suggestion that this was all the fault of the Stevens committee for having made him an "ultra-conservative"—this is so brazen as to border on the incredible.

The fearless vampire-killers

On the night of December 4, 1951, Eileen Tallman, an organizer for the United Steelworkers of America, and Lynn Williams, a young organizer for the CIO, sat over a beer in a tavern on Yonge Street, both in an elated mood.

On the same night, in the Eaton family home, Lady Eaton, John David Eaton, several directors and managers sat dispirited, waiting for the same moment.

Williams, now with the United Steelworkers of America in Toronto, recalled the night:

"We couldn't believe it had happened. We had been organizing for three years—it's impossible to describe the energy that went into that. Despite all the obstacles—the company propaganda campaign, the raises that were calculated to pull the rug from under us, the high turnover of staff—despite all that, Eileen and I were sure we had won. The managers were pretty depressed because they also thought we had won.

"That moment was the first hard lesson I got in labour organizing. So close . . ."

Out of 9914 Eaton's employees eligible to vote in the Toronto stores on whether or not to join a union, 4020 voted for the union, 4880 voted against and 259 ballots (mostly for the union) were spoiled.

The elation in the Eaton home, it is reported, was unbounded.

The Retail, Wholesale and Department Store Union (RWDSU) had begun organizing at Eaton's in Toronto during the summer of 1947. Because of the magnitude of the task—almost 10,000 workers of the 13,000 were eligible for unionization—a special committee of the Canadian Congress of Labour (affiliated with the CIO) was formed to organize the store into Local 1000.

"People's dissatisfaction," says Williams today, "was primarily over salaries—there were wide discrepancies between people who did essentially the same jobs. Women were paid much less than men for doing the same job.

"And there was the paternalism of the place—you had to make sure you were in the manager's favour or you were out, they controlled you completely, raises and promotions were not given on any general standard, but frequently on a totally preferential system."

Eaton's had not progressed far, in relative terms, since 1935. Not, at least, in wage terms. Here are rough average estimates from a salary survey done by union stewards at the time (bear in mind that these were wages recently hiked by general increases to throw the union off balance):

Group	Average Wage
Saleswomen in notions, stationery, etc. (with some years of seniority)	$36
Saleswoman, specialized selling (salary plus commission)	$40-44
Salesman, shoes, sporting goods and most straight salary departments	$55
Salesman, draperies, men's furnishings (salary plus commission)	$60-75

Starting rates were from $5 to $10 a week less. Different

rates applied according to age and marital and family status, even if for the same job.

The most salient feature of these wage rates was the much lower rates for women who might be doing the same job. Eaton's has not rushed to reform this aspect of their policy.

In the large restaurant departments, salaries were lower by $2 to $4 per week, and major grievances, according to union surveys, were "speed-up, layoffs, reducing employees' hours and job doubling... Older women are particularly insecure as when they become too slow they are got rid of in one way or another... a fair number of DPs (displaced persons—officialese for immigrants) are hired for food sections... Eatons' tries to make the DPs do more work than others."

In the mail-order department, unlike the showrooms which "are kept in a condition that is reasonably pleasant to the eye," things are "in a state of disrepair. The departments are completely void of air conditioning, with inadequate heat and fresh air for winter, and sweltering temperatures during the warm summer months..."

With these wages and conditions, however, Eaton's was not much worse than Simpson's or the entire retail industry. At the time, the retail field was the second-lowest paid among the nine leading industries in Canada. Industrial workers were largely organized; store employees were not. Thus the campaign to organize Eaton's held a prime importance to the whole labour movement—the Toronto stores were the key to organizing the retail industry, and the CCL spent $300,000 over three years trying to do it.

The campaign proceeded despite obstruction and red tape from the Ontario government on certification rights, despite turnover of staff and, most of all, despite the company counter-campaign.

Williams admits that the company fought back with a calculated, intelligent campaign that spared no costs either.

A group of employees "spontaneously" formed a counter-association called (shades of Lady Eaton's Mussolini days) "The Loyal Eatonians." Though the company insisted that it was not behind the formation of this curious loyalist movement, the group produced a series of slickly written pamphlets attacking the union that showed clear signs of company help.

Examples of the contents of some pamphlets:

"Why are these outsiders so concerned with your 'welfare'? They say they want you to enjoy the benefits and privileges they enjoy. Obviously they know little about you or this company!

"Obviously there is a lot more to this than warm, brotherly love.

"Let's do a little figuring:

"Local 1000's dues are now fixed at $1.50 a month. If they go no higher, the CIO could take no less than ... *$100,000 A YEAR OUT OF YOUR POCKETS!*

"If dues go up to $2.50 or $3.00 a month, as they have in many unions, the union take would be somewhere in the neighbourhood of . . . *$400,000 A YEAR!*

"Multiply that by the scores of department stores and thousands of retail outlets in Canada and you begin to get a glimpse of the rich prize the CIO is grasping for. You are the first step ...

"TO REPEAT:

"You are being asked to cast your whole future, your livelihood for yourself and your dependents, into the hands of strangers who lack any understanding of your work, your problems or your Company's, and whose motives are concealed behind exaggerated promises and carping criticism.

"Before you surrender your future into their hands, count what you have in benefits, rights, working conditions, opportunities and what you can reasonably hope to enjoy as the Company marches forward."

A pamphlet distributed November 13, 1951, a month before the vote, plays on the paranoia of the period. Under the title *"WHAT ARE THEY SELLING?"* they list:

COMMUNISM

"And communism has been an issue at least once [in the history of the CIO].

"Its crimson hue showed up in 1948 when the New York locals broke away from the RWDSU and the CIO. Their leaders could not, or would not, sign affidavits that they were NOT Communists as required under the U.S. Taft-Hartley labour law.

"Eventually, most of them did join a frankly Communist-led group. Macy's stayed out, however, but continued to conduct its business from the same lawyers' office as the Communist group."

Then the pamphlet cleverly lists all the names of the union executive, under the same heading as the above, leaving no doubt that these people are obviously Communists too.

Another pamphlet, entitled *"IT'S ALWAYS OPPORTUNITY DAY AT EATON'S,"* uses a Horatio Alger approach and tells the story of eleven directors and managers who clawed up through the ranks from stock boys and ledger-keepers.

But the company had an even more effective weapon to fight the union: money. The company did not intimidate employees, or fire union sympathizers. It simply brought in four general wage-hikes of $2 at three-month intervals, a pension plan and an improved welfare scheme—all much touted by the local press, which otherwise completely ignored the unionizing drive.

The post-mortem report done for the CIO attributes the defeat, by a margin of ten per cent, to "the anti-union campaign put on by the company during the final weeks of the vote" and the general wage increases. It concludes tersely—"and this line worked."

It did more than once.

John Deverell, a former employee of the wage administration office in the Winnipeg store, recalls being sent in 1964 to survey wages in the town of Dauphin, Manitoba, where Eaton's had a small store and restaurant. He had been sent on a routine survey of wages, and was about to report that he found them relatively geared to the local rates. But suddenly the Winnipeg office informed the Dauphin store that their wages were being hiked by "over $10 at least," according to Deverell.

"The reason was simple," he said. "It was explained to me by the chief wage administrator for Winnipeg and the western region, my boss, Garth Arnason. He said that a Dominion store had just been organized into the union in the same town, and there were many restaurant workers in that store too. The comparison in wage rates to Eaton workers would have been a little too obvious.

"So the salaries were immediately jacked to stave off any grounds for unionizing attempts by the employees.

"Arnason told me: any Eaton's wage administrator that

allows a union to be formed in his jurisdiction is immediately fired."

In 1970 the average wage of a saleswoman in the Toronto store was $1.70 an hour, and that of a salesman $2 an hour.

At the RWDSU office in the Ontario Federation of Labour building, they say "hundreds" of calls are received annually from Eaton's employees asking why there is no move to unionize them. They are regretfully told of 1951.

"It's hard to understand how we lost," Williams says today. "Maybe collective bargaining was not that accepted then. We came awfully close, nevertheless. It's the paternalism, though. And that's an elusive idea—how the men and women, the older ones of course, really believed all that Lady Eaton and the family-company stuff. They wanted to believe it. They gave them the frills and told them they were getting the substance.

"Eaton's is different, and more dangerous. That place was run on an ideology. It really controlled people.

"I remember we once put out a pamphlet on the Eaton mansion, and the incredible, gross luxuries in there. It was a castle, something out of another time. We thought the contrast to the working conditions would hit the workers, if we described this place.

"But I remember people really resented that piece. They really thought we should not have talked about the family, and their private place."

Sing Hallelujah and roll out the adjectives

Elevated to the status of a native aristocracy, possessed of one of the greatest fortunes in the country, close to the seats of power, the Eaton family and company were the object of a virtual conspiracy of silence by the press. And still are.

To this day, a story on Eaton's that deals with anything more than some trivia about Santa Claus parades must be passed through the highest editors of any of the English papers in Montreal, Toronto or Winnipeg. Assignments to cover Eaton events are generally assigned by the publisher or managing editor, with the addendum "Must Go."

In the *Montreal Gazette,* a reporter who wrote a humorous article on the Santa Claus parade of 1967 was banned by the then managing editor, John Meyer, from writing any articles not directly assigned by the editors, and from writing any features. He was informed that the article had angered Eaton's very much; that the publisher, Charles Peters, had received complaints from two Eaton's executives the day of the innocuous article's appearance; and that "this causes the *Gazette* great concern." Eaton's is one of the *Gazette's* major advertisers. The reporter was fired some weeks later.

The ban on mentioning Eaton's in any unfavourable light extends to the point that in court stories in the Toronto papers, if a shoplifter is tried for stealing from Eaton's, the store must not be named, but referred to as "a downtown department store."

The Eaton's main store in Toronto is right across Queen Street from Simpson's main store. Only a few years ago, when a hold-up man murdered a finance company manager downtown and fled through Eaton's lobby and then into Simpson's in an attempt to get lost in the crowd, the dramatic and sensational flight was described in one Toronto paper as being "through a downtown department store and south across Queen St. into another downtown department store."

During the startling testimony before the Stevens committee in 1935, all the Toronto papers produced the most incredible record of omissions in their coverage, which bears little relation to the actual testimony—not, at least, the damaging testimony.

The files of the Toronto and Montreal papers on Eaton's are replete with notices of their "generous donations to charity," "sparkling party," and "the family beloved by Canadians." In 1969, to honour the 100th anniversary of the store, both the *Toronto Telegram* and the *Toronto Star* ran multi-part series on the history of Eaton's, with sidelights about the family—a sycophancy rarely achieved even in the Canadian press.

This is not surprising, since it is commonly known that a vast part of the money that permitted John Bassett, then publisher of the *Telegram*, to keep the paper alive came from the Eaton family, and that the terms of succession for the *Telegram* specified that after Bassett's death or retirement the paper should be turned over to the sons of John Bassett and John David Eaton.

An idea of Eaton's continuing labour policy, and the

sycophancy of the Toronto press, comes from the following item which appeared in 1970 in the *New Lead*, house organ of the Toronto Newspaper Guild, the reporters' union:

Does anybody care?

EATON'S FIRES 200

Is it news that the T. Eaton Co. Ltd. is firing 200 maintenance employees?

The mighty retail chain is one of the biggest advertisers in the country.

What clout the ad dollar holds over local news media is debatable. But the Eaton story shows a tangible sensitivity in Toronto to the department store's power.

The first story written—and squelched—apparently was at the *Telegram*, and not surprisingly.

The Eaton family—mainly the founder's great-grandson—controls a large chunk of the *Tely* and of Baton Broadcasting Ltd., which owns television station CFTO [the *Telegram's* TV outlet in Toronto].

Briefly, the developments are that 196 maintenance workers at Eaton's downtown and College Street stores were to be taken off the payroll January 12.

The maintenance work is being contracted out to a private housekeeping concern, Consolidated Building Maintenance Ltd.

According to Eaton personnel chief Gordon Elliott, "10 to 20 per cent" of the laid-off employees will go to Consolidated—at lower pay than they were making at Eaton's . . . *Tely* reporter Marc Zwelling wrote the story on December 15, based on local labour-union sources.

He describes his story as "an interpretive piece" that revealed a drive had started by the Building Service Employees' International Union to organize the "new" Consolidated-Eaton workers.

It also pointed out the reduction in wages and the loss of the ten per cent Eaton employee discount suffered by the transferred workers.

It touched on the last big drive at Eaton's in 1953 [sic] and speculated that attempts might begin to carve out small bargaining units of catalogue employees, warehouse workers, truck drivers or restaurant workers.

"Oddly enough," says Zwelling, "the first tip I got on

the story was from *Tely* management. Simultaneously, I picked up the story from other sources."

Two days after he handed in his story, Zwelling was told the paper's "Eaton's censor" had vetoed it.

The Eaton dismissals did not die, however.

One of the fired caretakers, Mrs. Irene Goncher, went to see controller Margaret Campbell at her City Hall office on December 22 to try to enlist Mrs. Campbell's help.

Mrs. Goncher related to the City Hall press corps that "500 employees" had been laid off . . .

Again, a *Tely* reporter snapped at the story. Jake Calder of the paper's City Hall bureau filed a piece as a hard-news story, and it was quickly smothered.

By way of addendum, two days after this copy of *New Lead* was distributed within the newspapers, the *Star*, obviously goaded, ran a brief item, with no point of view of the workers quoted, on an inside page.

Telegram columnist Ron Haggart, the only journalist in Canada who ever successfully put Eaton's under a microscope, and who wrote in the *Telegram* under a great deal of editorial liberty, also wrote a column on this incident. The column was killed by his superiors.

But the silence that has reigned in the press around Eaton's is far from being a new phenomenon.

After referring to R.Y. Eaton's attempt to get a retraction from the *Telegram* for noting that Labour Day marchers dipped their flags as they passed Eaton's, Stephenson writes:

"Thereafter, Eaton's dealings with the fourth estate became virtually non-existent. Even journalists known to love and admire the firm found that they could not even interview the janitor. Anything Eaton's had to say to the Canadian public, R.Y. made it clear, would be said in its own advertisements . . ."

Eaton's stands as an untouchable, not required to reveal its assets, its business dealings, requiring a brown-nosing press to send its reporters as low-paid public-relations men to glorify any event Eaton's chooses to "suggest" to newspaper publishers they should cover. Even on the background of a Canadian press that has never shone for its daring or public responsibility, this stands as a monument of silence.

John David's little acre

The power Eaton's wields through its vast wealth, and the abandon with which the company exercises it, is illustrated by its massive land deals over the years.

In several cities Eaton's has amassed large segments of vital downtown land, kept it unused and frozen by not developing until it suited its purposes, and then forced local city councils into rezoning surrounding areas to accommodate the company's needs.

The most glaring example of this corporate citizen's behaviour, which casts further doubt on its "Greatest Good to the Greatest Number" myth, is to be found in Vancouver.

In March of 1948, Eaton's bought the old Hotel Vancouver on the city's main corner and unleashed its publicity machine with promises of building a huge department store that would transform the city centre. It demolished the ancient structure.

For the next twenty-two years, the site remained a vacant lot, used for parking, a gaping hole like a missing tooth in the centre of the city. For twenty-two years, the downtown development of Vancouver was stunted by the presence of this huge parking lot on Granville and Georgia. Eaton's was powerful and wealthy enough to do what almost no other corporation in the country can—hold on to critical development land against all pressures, public and otherwise, until it suited their own purposes to develop.

Finally in 1968, Eaton's, with its developer Cemp (owned by Seagram's liquor magnate Sam Bronfman), put it to the city of Vancouver: it would develop the square block if the city expropriated the block to the north and joined it to the Eaton complex. That block comprised ancient, family-owned businesses, small but not without charm. The city authorities were forced to go along with this economic blackmail, because Eaton's threatened not to develop that prime land unless it got what it wanted.

Furthermore, Eaton's played its old game of announcing its splendid plans in the press to whip up public enthusiasm, and then used that as leverage against any city authorities who had silly ideas about planned downtown development. In 1965, three years before the city capitulated, the *Vancouver Sun* ran a story familiar in other cities where Eaton's has done the same thing:

$20 MILLION TOWER PLANNED BY EATON'S

In April of 1964, the following headline in the *Toronto Star:*

EATON'S, ARGUS PLAN MAMMOTH DOWNTOWN PROJECT
$200 MILLION COMPLEX IN QUEEN-BAY AREA

And the following year:

MALLS, TOWERS AND SPACES IN EATON'S DOWNTOWN PLAN

Just one catch—Eaton's wanted the city of Toronto to turn over the old city hall building for demolition. This ancient, pseudo-gothic structure and clocktower is the only bit of colour and style to be found in the barren office-building face of downtown Toronto.

But again, through a publicity campaign in the press, through pressure on city hall, Eaton's got what it wanted. Then came the big surprise: Eaton's backed out because an economic survey it had done *after it had made all the plans and gotten what it wanted* showed that it would not make enough profit from the venture. The company told everybody to forget the whole thing.

Eaton's owns most of the property between Queen and College along the central downtown strip, and its old factories, offices and sweat shops have frozen all development of any significance in the surrounding area for decades.

In Montreal, Eaton's has a parking lot in the heart of the downtown area that blocks several arterial downtown routes, and leaves that area useless for development.

Another example of Eaton's hit-and-run project tactics is to be found in Hamilton. There, in 1955, the company arranged to buy Hamilton's city hall and some city land, on a promise to extend its store in two stages—one by 1957, another by 1962. A special law had to be passed by the Ontario legislature permitting Eaton's to go ahead with the deal. Unfortunately, Eaton's only completed the first part of the bargain, so the city passed a bylaw and the Ontario legislature passed another special law making it all legal and giving Eaton's a six-month extension.

Even that extension didn't prove sufficient. In 1963 the city council passed another three-year grace period, putting the deadline back to 1966.

Not even the Canadian Pacific Railway, the second-largest employer in the country, has been able to get away with keeping the grubby hands of public need and civic planning off its lands to the extent that the Eatons have with their leverage of wealth, influence and power.

The Kingdom and the Power and the Glory

The adjacent book department (in the Montreal store) is also huge, but may be moved to the fifth or sixth floor. The reason: so well-educated are today's Quebeckers that books are no longer the 'impulse buys' they once were, so need not be offered only on the hurried, helter-skelter main floor.
—The Store that Timothy Built, p. 169

"We always knew that Eaton's Santa was the real one, though," recalls Toronto-born Rick Rabin, now living in Gander. "You can't fool kids about anything as important as that."
—The Store that Timothy Built, p. 233

But what to do with her (a shoplifter) if she's caught? How to punish her without cutting the store off from all legitimate purchases she might make in the future—the dining-room and kitchen suites she'll need when she marries, the sheets, drapes, baby clothes, her husband's shoes, suits, guns and fishing rods?
—The Store that Timothy Built, p. 226

How does it fit? A company that has, admittedly, in the past led the way in such things as shorter hours and pension schemes, yet possesses a terror and hatred of unionism and collective bargaining unmatched by any corporation in Canada.

A family that has distributed millions through official charities, that builds churches and monuments and finances entire machine-gun batteries for the war, yet uses its financial leverage to work against the public good, control newspapers, and erect its splendid cathedral of opulence on a mountain of poor wages and arbitrary, dictatorial and paternalistic management.

A vast empire whose moguls steadfastly refuse to allow any encroachment of American capital. Sir John Craig Eaton, when questioned about rumours that the firm might sell to an American concern, declared expansively: "There is not sufficient money in the world to buy my father's name."

It fits well. For here is an empire—feudal in its myriad fiefdoms, in its stratified authority, its vassals and satrapies, crowned with an all-powerful gilded royalty. It is an empire with an ideology. Labour is not enough to earn the worker his wages—loyalty is required. Wealth is divine right. It is not a company, but a 'family'. (Employees were once called 'associates'.)

Its charities, apart from being convenient for tax purposes, are gifts from the king and queen, and the buildings and statues and church are monuments erected by them to the propagation of their own memory.

The Eatons were not interested only in making money. The Eatons wanted, and got, power, influence and—like all merchants who made their money in not the most glamorous field of capitalist endeavour—prestige and status. Lady Eaton is not an aberration, but the logical development of what this empire was founded on. Timothy Eaton built his empire on his life's savings. He didn't inherit it or even exploit it out of anyone—his first $6500 of capital were, to use a Calvinist phrase, 'reward for virtue'. And to use another Calvinist phrase, the Eatons are the 'elect'.

Profit is the prime goal, but not the only one. And once wealth is attained, as with the Carnegie and Rockefeller fortunes, come philanthropy and sponsorship of the arts, and the titles. Above all, rich and powerful, the Eatons wanted to be respected, even loved by the little people of Canada.

But Eaton's never lost sight of the dollar all the while the family was pursuing prestige. In a manner that is truly mercantile genius, they devised the Career Girls' Clubs, the Junior Councils of clean-cut high-school boys and girls, the Santa Claus parades. One wonders they never got into pee-wee hockey.

In places Eaton's has successfully resisted history—it built an empire entirely on indigenous capital, contemptuous of the crass profit-making-only corporations that wiped out all the other Eatons of Canadian commercial and industrial history. It also resisted the labour-union movement with a tenacity that spared no expense, and created its own internal welfare state to buttress its authority. Like an ancient institution that history long ago decreed should have died, or at least transformed, it maintains its stresses within, in order to resist change.

The oft-expressed proposition that "Eaton's is Canada" is a facile caricature. But Eaton's is something that grew in a manner peculiar to Canada, and it stands as a Canadian institution, the highest development of Canadian capital. It is a museum piece in a day of pleasant young men from New York and branch-plant managers.

Those who seek truly Canadian institutions today should not tarry before coming upon this monument to what our native wealth and power has erected. And may it be a sobering discovery.

Why the CPR Doesn't Like You
by Robert Chodos

"The train's pretty full tonight," said one conductor to another as the Canadian Pacific Railway's sleek *Canadian* headed through the smoky industrial area of Montreal towards Windsor Station, coming in from Ottawa on the final leg of its transcontinental trip.

"It usually is," said the other conductor. "They could fill another Ottawa-Montreal train too if they scheduled it properly. But they won't."

"It doesn't make any sense," agreed the first conductor. "Crazy company we work for."

If they thought that their employer had lost the business acumen and eye for profit that had built it into a conglomerate with a net income of $80 million a year, they needn't have worried. For making money on its passenger services is not part of Canadian Pacific's grand design. In fact, on some of its passenger runs, it is to the ultimate corporate benefit of Canadian Pacific to lose as much money as it can.

It has been a long time since the CPR has even made any pretence of wanting to be in the passenger business. In 1965 the late Robert A. Emerson, then CPR president, said that he could "see no prospect of being able to attract to passenger trains people in sufficient numbers at prices they are willing to pay to defray the expenses incurred," and every CPR executive who has felt it necessary to express himself on the subject of passengers has echoed that position. However, Emerson and his successors have sometimes tried to give the impression that they have tried everything to make rail travel attractive, only to be spurned by an unappreciative public. The facts are somewhat different.

Under the National Transportation Act, passed by the Pearson government in 1967, a railway wishing to abandon a passenger service or branch line must first prove that it is los-

*Published in the *Last Post*, September 1970.

ing money on the service to the satisfaction of the Canadian Transport Commission, the body set up by the government to administer transportation policy. Then the CTC, after considering "all matters that in its opinion are relevant to the public interest," will rule on whether the railway can go ahead and abandon it. If it rules that it is not in the public interest for the service to be abandoned, the railway must keep it going and the government will subsidize its losses on the service to the extent of eighty per cent.

Two years after the act was passed, the railways made their first applications for abandonment. The government-owned Canadian National Railways applied to abandon thirteen of its passenger runs, mostly serving out-of-the-way towns where there are few, if any, alternatives to rail transportation. The CPR applied to abandon its entire passenger service except for its Montreal commuter routes.

The CTC is expected, although not required, to hold public hearings on applications for abandonment (Transport Minister Don Jamieson assured the House of Commons in the fall of 1969 that everyone would get a chance to say his piece, noting that under the National Transportation Act, "the public interest is quite well protected"), and it decided to begin in Guelph and Owen Sound, Ontario, with hearings on the abandonment of passenger links between those communities and Toronto.

From the railways' point of view, the experiment with public hearings was a disastrous failure. University professors, housewives, students, provincial government economists and commuters all turned up with evidence that service should be continued.

The CPR decided that, in its next move, it should proceed with somewhat more circumspection. In cancelling three of its five Ottawa-Montreal trains, it would make sure that it had built up an incontrovertible case that the runs were uneconomic. And it would, if possible, try to avoid public hearings.

To achieve its first goal, it rescheduled its trains to make them as inconvenient as possible. A morning train was pushed forward from 8 am to 11:30 am, to render it useless for people who wanted to make a one-day trip. An evening train from Ottawa to Montreal was rescheduled to pass through

Montreal West station at 9:50—missing a connection for New York by five minutes.

Meal service was curtailed, and prices were raised. A bacon-and-eggs breakfast that had cost $1.95 now cost $2.75 à la carte (including 20 cents for toast, 30 cents for marmalade or jam and 40 cents for tea or coffee).

CPR trains, instead of attracting an average of 150 customers, now attracted an average of 40.

Then the railway, complaining that it was losing money, announced that it would cut out three trains daily in each direction on August 1, 1970, leaving only the Montreal-Ottawa leg of the *Canadian* and one other train in service. And since this was only a reduction of service and not a discontinuance, it claimed the right to do this without getting permission from the CTC.

The CTC and its chairman Jack Pickersgill agreed to the CPR's definition of its powers. It raised no objection to the dropping of the Montreal-Ottawa trains, although there were outcries from everyone from the Canadian Railway Labour Association to the *Montreal Star*.

Meanwhile, a larger battle was shaping up. Among the trains the CPR had applied to discontinue was the *Canadian*, the last remnant of its once-proud transcontinental service. The CTC said no and told the CPR to prepare a "rationalization" plan to cut the *Canadian's* losses. The CPR's plan, submitted on July 20, 1970, the deadline given by the CTC, included reducing the *Canadian* to three days a week except in peak periods, and cutting out dining and sleeping-car service. Again, customers would be driven away and it would be only a matter of time before the *Canadian* was dropped completely.

Unable to escape public hearings, the CTC proceeded to schedule them for the most inconvenient possible time—mid to late August, when many people would be on vacation, when farmers would be out harvesting and before anyone except the CPR would have had time to prepare briefs.

Faced with protests over the timing, Pickersgill, who hadn't spent half his life with the likes of Mackenzie King and Paul Martin without learning how to weasel out of an uncomfortable situation, said the possibility of holding hearings at places east of Winnipeg had been under study and, in order to provide the sixty-day postponement requested by anyone with reasonable grounds for a delay, the commission was willing to hold additional hearings after the end of September. However, "the Commission has decided to proceed with the hearings as announced, in order to give Canadian Pacific an opportunity to elaborate on its proposals, to be questioned on them, and to enable other parties to proceed with their submissions, if they are ready to do so." On the key question of whether additional hearings would be held in the West, Pickersgill said nothing.

The CPR's tactics, and the government's docility, were a familiar story. For the CPR had once had three daily transcontinental trains. One was dropped in 1959, and in August 1965 the railway announced that it would drop a second one, the *Dominion*, on September 7. The Board of Transport Commissioners, predecessor to the CTC, issued an order on September 1 that "the Canadian Pacific Railway Company shall continue to operate the present passenger service provided by the *Dominion* until the Board orders otherwise."

Prevented from dropping the *Dominion*, the CPR did the next best thing. The *Dominion* that left Montreal for Vancouver on September 7, 1965, had no sleeping cars or dining cars—it consisted of an engine, a baggage car, and two coaches. Passengers stayed away in droves. On September 28, the CPR again asked for permission to drop the *Dominion*. Again, the BTC said no.

At subsequent public hearings, the BTC was faced with unkind remarks about the way the CPR had "complied" with its order. Chief Commissioner Rod Kerr replied that "the basic purpose of the Board Order was to continue the *Dominion*. Seasonal changes in the consist of the train have been made from time to time and the Board did not treat the Order, regardless of the fact that it was and is susceptible perhaps to a different interpretation, the Board did not treat the Order as precluding the company from initiating such changes, such seasonal changes."

Meanwhile, the CPR claimed that it had to cancel the *Dominion* because it needed the diesel power to haul the wheat that the Canadian government had just sold to the Soviet Union. This, however, was evidently an afterthought, since even CPR president Emerson admitted that "before advice was received by Company officers from the Government of the proposed increase in wheat sales to Russia, plans for the discontinuation of the *Dominion* were well under way, although no decision had been announced."

On January 7, 1966, the BTC authorized the CPR to drop the *Dominion*. By January 11, the *Dominion* had vanished without a trace. The Board said it might require the CPR to revive the *Dominion* for the busy summer season, or perhaps for the Centennial travel boom in 1967, but it never did.

"My politics? Railways are my politics!"
—Sir Allan MacNab, Prime Minister of Canada, 1854

Friendship and co-operation between the Canadian Pacific Railway and the government of Canada are not recent innovations. For the building of the CPR in the 1880s was not the work of a small group of entrepreneurs acting alone. It was a public project, paid for largely by the Canadian people. It was the centre-pin in the vision of a native Canadian capitalist class just recently come to life and soon to die in infancy. Prussia under Frederick the Great was said to have been not a state with an army, but an army with a state. Canada in the 1880s was not a country with a railway, but a railway with a country.

The building of the CPR was the climax of a railway boom that had begun twenty years earlier, when Canadian businessmen-politicians has stopped simply granting land to each other and started granting railway charters as well. The origins of that boom were not in any move to create an independent Canadian economy. In 1849, Montreal's leading capitalists had signed a manifesto that Canada be annexed by the United States, and the first railways were built in that same spirit.

Their purpose was to provide convenient routes between the fast-growing American West and east-coast ports in the United States. The Grand Trunk Railway, the high point of this first orgy of Canadian railway building (2000 miles of road were constructed between 1850 and 1860), ran from southern Ontario through Montreal to Portland, Maine. The Grand Trunk specialized in good relations with guardians of the public purse: several leading citizens of the 1850s simultaneously held executive positions in the Grand Trunk Railway, the Bank of Montreal and the government of Canada.

Another Grand Trunk potentate was Alexander Tilloch Galt, commissioner of the British-American Land Company, who considered "the interests of the Company and of the country to be identical."

With government loans of £3000 per mile of road built (Canada's public debt increased from $12 per capita in 1852 to $30 per capita in 1867, almost entirely as a result of railway building), the Grand Trunk prospered. And so, almost despite itself, did native Canadian industry. For although the railway boom began in response to American needs, it could not but help spark an industrial revolution in Canada—first the building of railway equipment, then other industries, started to spring up. A proposal for a political unification of the colonies, which held out the promise of a common market and the possibility of more railways, sprang up with it. The railway-promoter/banker/politicians would soon be seen in yet another guise: Fathers of Confederation.

Galt joined the cabinet of Georges-Etienne Cartier (also a Grand Trunk man) and John A. Macdonald in 1858 as finance minister, exacting a promise that the government embody in its program a proposal for a federal union of Canada, the Maritimes and the Northwest Territories.

When Canada and the Maritimes united in 1867, the links were to be secured by the long-awaited Intercolonial Railway, to bring Maritime resources down to Upper Canada. Some, however, entertained a still wider vision. Manitoba and the Northwest Territories entered Confederation in 1870, and when British Columbia was negotiating entry a year later, its delegation—made up of representatives of British capital and Canadian investors—demanded a wagonroad to the Pacific as a condition of union. The easterners promised them something even better: a railway.

Prime Minister Sir John A. Macdonald immediately set about fulfilling the promise. He awarded the contract to a syndicate called the Canadian Pacific Railway Company, headed by Sir Hugh Allan of Montreal, along with a subsidy of $30 million in cash and 50 million acres of land along the main line, plus additional land subsidies for the branches. But when it was revealed that Sir Hugh had enriched the coffers of Sir John A.'s Conservative Party by $300,000, the Pacific railway project and the Macdonald government both came crashing down.

The succeeding Reform administration of Alexander Mackenzie was not nearly as committed to building railways. And besides, the boom-and-bust economic cycle had just entered one of its prolonged busts. Railway building under Mackenzie was limited to the construction, as government projects, of lines where no water transportation was available. But with the upturn in the economy in 1878 and the return of the Conservatives in the elections of that year, interest in the idea of a Pacific railway revived. Within three years, a new Canadian Pacific Railway Company had been formed.

The new syndicate, headed by Montreal financiers George Stephen (later Lord Mount Stephen) and Donald Smith (later Lord Strathcona and Mount Royal), avoided the mistakes of the old. The government chipped in with a grant of $25 million and 25 million acres of land. As well, it turned over to the CPR the lines that had been built under the Mackenzie administration at a cost of $38 million. Far-reaching tax exemptions were thrown in too, along with a provision that the company would have a monopoly of western traffic for twenty years.

In return, the CPR promised "the completion and perpetual and efficient operation of the railway."

British and French backing was rounded up for the project. William Van Horne was brought in from the United States to run the show. Immigrants were brought in from Europe to do the actual work—cheaply. More government assistance was repeatedly asked for (the company was constantly on the verge of bankruptcy) and obtained. By 1885, less than five years after it had started construction, the CPR had fulfilled the first part of its bargain. The last spike was driven in at Craigellachie, and the railway was completed. In June 1886, service was begun between Montreal and Port Moody, BC, fourteen miles east of Vancouver.

But already the company had more than a railway. It had the land (total grants in the end came to 36,370,828 acres, by the company's own figures), which it gradually sold off to settlers and land companies, carefully retaining the rights to the minerals underneath. It bought its first steamships in 1884, and opened its first hotels in 1886. (Its hotels now include the Empress in Victoria, the Saskatchewan in Regina, the Royal York in Toronto, the Château Champlain in Montreal and the Château Frontenac in Quebec City.)

When the CPR wanted to buy a railway charter in the Crow's Nest Pass area from one F. Augustus Heinze in the 1890s, it found that a smelter at Trail came as part of the bargain. To keep the smelter going, it began to buy mines in the area, eventually acquiring the Sullivan Mine at Kimberley, BC, now one of the world's largest lead-zinc mines. The mining and smelting properties grew into the giant Consolidated Mining and Smelting Company (Cominco), 53 per cent owned by Canadian Pacific. In the 1920s people began to complain that sulphur from the smelter at Trail was killing vegetation in the area, and when the complaints started becoming lawsuits the company decided to recover the sulphur instead, and went into the fertilizer business. It now also has a potash mine near Saskatoon, a 69 per cent share of the rich Pine Point mine in the Northwest Territories, a 9.03 per cent share of Panarctic Oils Ltd., now busily engaged in drilling for oil in the Canadian north (Canadian Pacific Oil and Gas, another CPR subsidiary, has an additional 9.03 per cent share), and mining and manufacturing operations in Japan, India and the United States among its diverse interests.

The company's entry into oil and gas came much later. Oil was discovered on its property at Leduc, Alberta, in 1947, but it had leased the land to oil companies and cashed in primarily in the form of rents, reservation fees and production royalties. In the late fifties it began its own drilling program in Alberta, and in 1964 began to explore for oil and gas in the North Sea off Great Britain.

Marathon Realty, yet another subsidiary, owns Place du Canada in Montreal, Palliser Square in Calgary, Project 200 in Vancouver and industrial parks in Montreal, Sudbury, Calgary and Edmonton. Pacific Logging Co. Ltd. carries out logging operations on Vancouver Island and operates a lumber-processing complex in the Kootenays.

CP Air began as a small feeder operation but, with a government only too willing to grant it lucrative routes, now has passenger revenues of more than $100 million a year, with flights from Canada to Australia, Holland, southern Europe and Latin America. In 1958 it was first allowed into the rich transcontinental domestic market—until then the exclusive preserve of the publicly owned Air Canada—with one flight a day, which the Air Transport Board justified on the grounds of linking its international gateway terminals. By 1970, CP Air had seven transcontinental 'executive jets' daily.

By 1962, Canadian Pacific interests had become so widespread that a separate company, Canadian Pacific Investments, was set up to manage the non-transportation part of the operation. The net income of Investments in 1968 was $41,902,000.

By contrast, the CPR's *total* income from rail passenger transportation in that year was $13,421,720.

"The public generally, and businessmen specifically, must come to realize that it is just as moral and just as praise-worthy to operate a railway, an airline, or a trucking firm at a profit as it is to make a profit manufacturing motor cars or packing meat or making steel."
—Hon. Jack Pickersgill, June 9, 1970

On October 28, 1960, Robert Emerson, then a CPR vice-president, appeared before the MacPherson Royal Commission on Transportation to present the railway's brief on passenger service. Emerson said that the CPR firmly opposed the idea of maintaining unprofitable passenger runs or branch lines by federal subsidies; he called it a "flagrant misuse" of federal money to perpetuate these "uneconomic" services (the irony of the CPR's coming out against federal subsidies has been noted).

And the only thing that was preventing the railways from getting rid of passenger services as they wished was public opinion.

"The passenger deficit," Emerson said, "is a problem which is within the power of railway management to rectify, given a realistic public climate and reasonable regulation."

He called for legislation to permit the railways to get rid of losing passenger or branch-line facilities without a major fuss from the communities affected. He insisted that "passenger train service on Canadian Pacific is no longer required for the economic well-being of Canada."

The MacPherson Report, presented to the government in 1961, did not embody all the CPR's proposals.

It did, however, accept their basic philosophy, which saw

that railways were to be operated for profit. It suggested that the government should largely keep its nose out of the transportation business, and that "competition" should be the main regulatory factor.

This was, in effect, a ratification of a CPR corporate policy that had let passenger equipment deteriorate while pouring capital into freight equipment and drilling for oil, because that was where the profits were to be made.

But not quite. The MacPherson Report did not totally abandon the proposition that the railways had a public service to provide. It recommended, for instance, that the government control railway freight rates in cases where shippers had no other recourse (although it suggested the removal of all other freight rate controls—freight revenues of both major railways have shot up since the MacPherson Report was implemented in the National Transportation Act of 1967). And it also recommended that the government subsidize passenger routes and branch lines that could not possibly make money but are necessary for the public interest.

On the whole, however, the MacPherson Report corresponded to what the railways wanted, and the railways were happy with it.

Nevertheless, it was at this time that Canadian National Railways embarked on a challenge to the established truth that railway passenger service was a moribund institution. The CNR had always been something of an ugly stepsister to Canadian Pacific: it had started life in 1919 when the government took over two bankrupt railways, the Grand Trunk Pacific and the Canadian Northern. A few years later, the government tacked on the venerable Grand Trunk Railway, which had also fallen on hard times, and other smaller roads. It was not until the post-war regime of Donald Gordon, when a massive modernization program was undertaken, that the CNR became anything like an efficient, productive railway.

There has always been a certain ambiguity surrounding the nature of the CNR: its executives, by and large, have regarded it as a business to be run like any other, but it was impossible to escape entirely the idea that, as a publicly owned utility, the CNR had a responsibility to the public as well as to itself. And the same ambiguity pervaded the heresy that the CNR proclaimed in the 1960s. In a speech to the Moncton Board of Trade in 1965, Pierre Delagrave, then vice-president for passenger sales and services, said that "I cannot stress too strongly that CN is in the passenger business to make a profit—sooner or later." But in the same speech he admitted that the best CN might be able to do was break even, or cut its losses to a minimum. Nobody at CN ever expected to reach the break-even point before the early 1970s.

At any rate, CN plunged into the passenger business head first. It reduced fares drastically on many runs. In 1962, it introduced its red, white and blue-fare plan, with cheaper fares on non-peak travel days, in the Maritimes. The experiment was a success, and the next year it expanded red, white and blue to include the whole system. When in 1965 the CPR pulled out of pool-train agreements in the Montreal-Ottawa-Toronto triangle, CN introduced its Rapido—Montreal to Toronto non-stop in five hours. The ill-starred Turbotrain, when it functioned properly, reduced travel time by yet another hour. Bistro cars with live entertainment, computerized reservations and heavy, heavy advertising were further innovations.

The response was encouraging. The number of passengers carried jumped by 14 per cent in the single year between 1963 and 1964. Passenger revenues rose from $48 million in 1961 to $84 million in 1967.

Meanwhile, Ian Sinclair, the CPR's new president, sat back and said "I think they are wrong. Based on all the information I have and based on all the judgements I can give it, we know they are wrong."

In CN's top management, the faction that agreed with Sinclair was winning out. Pierre Delagrave, the most enthusiastic supporter of passenger service and the architect of CN's passenger policy, left the railway in late 1965 for Domtar Ltd. By May 1969, Robert Bandeen, CNR vice-president for corporate planning and finance, was saying that continuing passenger rail service in Canada "doesn't make any economic sense." He called the subsidies paid the railways by the federal government a glaring example of wasted financial resources in the transportation industry, and said the CNR and the CPR should get out of the passenger business.

How large a part the passage of the National Transportation Act in 1967 played in this change in CN policy is not clear. The MacPherson Report, the basis for the act, was supported by CN top executives, including Delagrave, even while the passenger experiment was in full swing.

However, the act was the product of the same kind of thinking as the new CN policy—the same kind of thinking that could allow Robert Emerson, when reminded of his company's pledge of "perpetual and efficient operation of the railway" during the hearings on the *Dominion* in 1965, to say that "efficient operation" meant "profitable operation."

In the new era of railways-for-profit, the chief guardian of the public interest was to be the Canadian Transport Commission, set up under the act. Those who hoped the CTC would perform that function effectively were not reassured when transport minister Jack Pickersgill, who had just helped create the $40,000-a-year job of CTC chairman, promptly appointed himself to fill it. They have been further dismayed by the commission's polite attitude towards the railways.

Perhaps the most disturbing thing of all was Pickersgill's remarkable speech of June 9, 1970, to the Canadian Manufacturers' Association in Montreal.

It was that speech which prompted Maurice Wright, lawyer for the Canadian Railway Labour Association, to bring the August 17 Winnipeg hearing on the *Canadian* to a halt with a demand (rejected by the courts) that Pickersgill be disqualified from participating in the hearings. The CTC chairman, Wright said, had clearly shown his bias in favour of the railways.

In the June 9 speech, Pickersgill emphasized the need to get rid of "uneconomic services and facilities which are no longer required in the public interest."

He called this "a process which is going to be painful in the short run, but highly beneficial to the public and the treasury in the longer run.

"To be carried out successfully, public understanding and support for the process of rationalization and modernization will be indispensable."

Familiar sentiments when spoken by CPR and, latterly, CNR executives, but more worthy of attention when coming from a guardian of the public interest: "It is essential that, so far as possible, transport services be operated on business-like lines with economic viability as the main test of efficiency and adequacy."

Meanwhile, some people began to insist on other criteria for the value of passenger services than the CPR's profit margins.

At the Guelph hearings in April 1970, Kirk Foley, a transportation economist with the Ontario government, demonstrated that if the Guelph-Toronto run were discontinued, Ontario would have to make an *immediate* expenditure of $4 million on roads to prevent the level of highway service from seriously degenerating. And further expenditures would be necessary in the future.

Foley also pointed out that the government of Canada runs its 190 airports at an annual deficit of $57 million. As well, it spends $121 million a year for communication, navigational aids and meteorological services—a large proportion of which can be regarded as a direct subsidy to airlines.

This suggests that the government is subsidizing airlines to an extent exceeding the $68 million it will hand over to the railways in 1970. And this does not take into account the losses the government will take on the $644-million cost of the new Montreal international airport at Ste-Scholastique and the $200 to $300-million cost of expanding the Toronto international airport.

Nor, in terms of total expenditure of resources, does it take into account the tax loss on underused lands around airports, or the distortion of highway needs that airports entail.

Rail transportation can also be offered at a much lower price than air travel; when a Turbotrain is in full operation, its per-seat running cost is one-third that of an airplane. It is not the poor who will benefit from the new international airports.

Another witness at Guelph, landscape architect William Coates, pointed to the horrible example of San Francisco:

"In the middle 1950s, a good, high-speed electric railway, the Key system, served the eastern side of the San Francisco Bay area connecting the cities of Berkeley and Oakland with San Francisco. Local authorities allowed this line to suspend operations in response to financial pressures and the entire system was dismantled.

"Invaluable right-of-way property was sliced up like so

much sausage and sold piecemeal. Private automobiles and buses fulfilled the need and contributed to the growing smog blanket. In 1962, seven years later, the electorate of the same area, strangling on exhaust fumes, inadequate freeways and limited parking in San Francisco, voted a $792-million bond issue to build a new high-speed electric railway, the Bay Area Rapid Transit, to service the same area plus some new communities. A substantial portion of the $792 million was used to buy new rights-of-way along original Key route lines.

"This was anything but common-sense, comprehensive long-range planning."

One well-known fact about the automobile is its insatiability. Studies done in the early sixties showed that land used for a four-track railway would provide seven times more passenger-miles than if the same land were used for a four-lane highway.

In the United States, where the automobile is king, Congress authorized the $41-billion interstate highway system in 1956. With only 70 per cent of the system completed, $41 billion has already been spent and Congress will soon authorize an additional $34 billion for interstate highways. The U. S. National Organization of State Highway Officials estimates that "the national highway needs for the next 15 years will cost $320 billion."

Meanwhile, other countries are demonstrating the advantages of rail-passenger transport. In France, electric trains run at average speeds of 65 miles an hour. In Britain, upgraded train service between major cities has resulted in a 60 per cent increase in rail passengers. Japanese "Bullet" trains travelling at more than 130 mph carry 200,000 passengers a day in the heavily populated Tokyo-Nagoya-Osaka areas.

In Australia, the state railway system of New South Wales carries 233 million commuters and 15 million long-distance travellers yearly. "We don't really expect to make profits from passengers," says Neal McCusker, head of the New South Wales system. "We make money from hauling freight and have a responsibility to the public to provide comfortable transport and an efficient commuter service at a reasonable cost."

All of which suggests that a comprehensive rail-passenger system might be highly "economic" and "efficient" for

Canada, if not for the CPR. This has been the basic point made by the Canadian Railway Labour Association, uniting several railway unions, in its fight against rail-passenger abandonment. Its efforts have included participation in public hearings and a campaign to bring the issue to the attention of the public.

One person who was disturbed when the MacPherson Report was issued in 1961 was Jean Marchand, then president of the Confederation of National Trade Unions and now federal minister of Regional Economic Expansion.

"Transportation policy," Marchand said, "is closely tied to economic planning and as such must be linked to the common good and not the profitability of private enterprise."

Try to tell that to the CPR, or to Jack Pickersgill.

Why the Farmer's Dying
by Ralph Surette

The year is 1961. Communist Plots rustle in the wheat fields like Riel's ghost. That is to be expected. But who would have suspected one lurking beneath the Peace Tower itself, disguised as a civilized scheme of rural development in the very bosom of the Conservative Party?

The Liberal mandarins, waiting impatiently for their true masters to return to power, are distraught. Is Alvin Hamilton, John Diefenbaker's radical-Tory Agriculture minister, really a Saskatchewan Commie?

On January 26 of that year Hamilton announces ARDÁ, the Agricultural Rehabilitation and Development Act. It is the most ambitious scheme ever to attempt to rehabilitate Canada's decaying rural lifestyles. Its fulcrum will be local participation. The farmer will have a say in his own affairs. Co-operatives will be formed.

"It must be a co-operative enterprise of governments, groups and individuals," Hamilton says. "This would also include the churches." It is to be a total-concept approach as prevails in countries where agriculture actually works. It will involve the development of all local resources, including such things as forestry, recreation lands, tourist facilities and common community pastures.

Alas, poor Alvin. He thought he could deviously sidestep the private sector just like that—not to mention the Liberal mandarins—and get away with it.

The Forces of Freedom were vigilant.

ARDA'S militants were undercut by people in government as well as by the white-gloved technocrats who considered the plan 'socialist'.

ARDA'S most ambitious program was for the Lower St. Lawrence River area. The Créditistes, who in many cases represented the counties that needed it most, scurried around denouncing it as—what else?—a Communist Plot.

*Published in the *Last Post*, November 1971.

Exit Alvin the Red.

A lot of farmers have gone under since ARDA tried and failed. Those who remain in business, especially the small and marginal ones, do so in fear, anger and a heightened awareness of their condition in the face of the Trudeau government's determination to wipe them out in favour of corporate agribusiness.

Ten years later, an epochal barrier was crossed by the collective rural psyche. In late August of 1971, farmers in Prince Edward Island blocked the island's main drag with their tractors for a week in protest against policies favouring corporate farming. National Farmers' Union president Roy Atkinson, leading the men, was arrested for "conspiracy to intimidate."

That this could happen in slow-moving PEI after several years of mounting protests in the rest of Canada—very bitter ones in Ontario (produce giveaways), Manitoba (tractor blockades) and Saskatchewan (rotten wheat in Trudeau's face)—is like the last piece falling into a jigsaw puzzle. If there was a last bastion of mildew-and-rubber-boots conservatism in Canada, then surely it must have been PEI.

What ARDA tried to be, what it actually became, why it failed and how the thread of that failure led many rural people to the brink of revolt a decade later says a lot of nasty and interesting things about the Canadian power structure.

But first here is the wider background of the present unrest.

Rural depopulation—the backside of urbanization—has been a way of life in Canada for a long time. In 1872 over three-quarters of the population lived in the countryside. In 1972, three-quarters live in the cities.

The country boy's trek to the city is one of the prime equations of our social history. It is intimately linked with the centralizing process of technology and capitalism—the drawing of wealth to the centres of power and the resulting unemployment in the hinterland.

Centralization's first big send-off occurred in Canada when Confederation was imposed on unwilling Maritimers, draining the wealth of thriving localized economies into the coffers of Upper Canadian bankers. The Maritimes have since remained the major economic backwater of vice-imperial central Ontario, its more unfortunate children becoming immigrants in their own country.

Except for specific cases, the migrations—especially since the Second World War—were not always a painful thing, as populations became more mobile and going places was in the wind. True, many didn't make it past the urban slums or the mines of industrial Ontario. But some floated into the urban middle class. Some returned home. It was generally accepted that one son would take over the farm and the nine others would leave, as local economies absorbed only what they could.

There was always some protest against this over the years, but it never congealed on a national scale. It was Progress—one of the unquestionable official myths. The centralizing process of capitalism seemed natural, up to a point—and that point has now been passed.

The relatively self-sufficient prairie communities strung out along the railway one hundred years ago were defined by how far a horse could travel in a day. These were superseded by communities whose influence was defined by the distances of the motor car, the local telephone exchange and hydro wires.

Technology, capitalist or not, would probably have brought about these changes. The kid from Naicam, Sask., who learned a specialized skill would have moved to Melfort or on to Saskatoon or Regina anyway (although it must be added that in North American-style business there was always an excess of cheap rural labour drawn to the cities through the essential fraud of neon lights and Hollywood's public relations for the system).

What is happening now is infinitely more serious, as the natural centralizing effect of mere technological development has long since been bypassed. To complete the example of Saskatchewan, the drain does not consist of Naicam's young bloods being drawn to Saskatoon, but large numbers of people from the entire province—rural and urban—fleeing out of the province pursued by joblessness. This issue was central in the provincial election that saw the NDP wipe out the Liberals with slogans based on Statistics Canada figures such as "last year three people left Saskatchewan every hour, 72 every day, 500 every week, 20,000 in the year."

Sometime in the mid-sixties, with the Liberals in power to

whom the outback is merely a place for minor patronage, the strains on rural Canada became unbearable, as Canada's rate of urbanization became one of the highest in the world.

Competition capitalism was becoming more clearly monopoly and multinational and seemed to be moving into a final stage of frenzied centralism to be capped off by a continental energy package. Canada's role as an economic satellite of the US became more clearly defined, and its own internal economic centralism increased accordingly.

It must be said that the farmer has been generally more sensitive to this trend than the urban person, not only because he was one of its first victims but because he is less influenced by the obscurantist metropolitan media.

Thus the 1970 royal commission report by Dr. Clarence Barber revealing that multinational corporations—Massey Ferguson, Ford, International Harvester, John Deere, David Brown and British Leyland Motors—were bilking Canadian farmers of as much as $2000 extra per tractor, while it surprised many urban people, only confirmed the obvious for the farmers.

Members of the Ontario Federation of Agriculture knew it better than anyone. The OFA had been importing tractors from England with great difficulty and at half the Canadian price—and had to weld steel plates over the serial numbers to protect the British retailer. However Dr. Barber reported that some of these steel plates had been pried off in the night when the tractors arrived at the port of Montreal, presumably by the multinationals' 'secret agents'.

Economic centralism is not without its political wing—the Trudeau government, carrying on the traditional role of the Liberal Party but with that peculiar incontinence that one columnist, referring to the party's place on the political spectrum, called "extremism at the centre."

The federal government has, in fact, decided to institutionalize rural depopulation by reducing the farm population from the present ten per cent to three per cent by 1990 as recommended by the 1968 Task Force on Agriculture—a veritable behemoth of reasoning in favour of technocratic centralism written by four professors and an accountant. Without farmer representation, naturally.

It is argued that, since one-third of Canadian farmers are chronically on or below the poverty line, they should be replaced by corporate farming and retrained to work in industry.

The government's policy includes the following options: A farmer who has reached retirement age can get a government allowance which, along with the sale of his farm, the government presumes will afford him a decent living.

A younger man can go into a manpower retraining program, although there are no special programs designed specifically for farmers.

A farmer whose operations can become profitable, in the government's judgement, will be given assistance in buying out his neighbours. That is, to become a corporation. The bigger the better.

The policy's deficiencies are too obvious to bother repeating at length. Poor farmers are going to be retrained for urban jobs that do not exist. And viable communities that, except for the native peoples, represent the most durable and indigenous way of life that has existed in this country will be destroyed with cavalier insouciance.

There is no need to rationalize the knowledge that farmers have in their gut. Suffice it to say that a number of socio-economic studies support their point, the latest being one called the Prairie Community System, a publication of the Agricultural Economics Research Council of Canada. This is a thoroughly apolitical document by Professor Carle Zimmerman, an American mostly connected with Harvard but recently of the University of Calgary, and his associate, Garry Moneo of Saskatchewan.

They state that Canada is simply repeating policies that were tried in the US ten years ago and failed at enormous cost. The study also emphasizes the value of small communities which counterbalance the technological excesses of our society, and it notes a trend in which Westerners are "trying to organize a folk life to make the Prairies more of a Canadian homeland."

The picture of rural Canada being screwed becomes morbidly complete when one considers that speculators are carrying out a massive grab of recreational lands in Canada, mostly for resale to Americans. Not only are farmers to be cleared off the land to make way for the corporations, but in true imperial style the land is to be divided, with the best of

Ralph Surette / 53

it becoming the summer estates of the genteel absentee landlords.

This has already happened to a large extent. In the Maritimes especially, where it was never assumed that ownership of land meant you could prevent the other guy from walking across it, the neighbourly Maritimers are extremely uptight these days about all those "keep out" signs defacing the land—sure sign of the moneyed American with a keen sense of the meaning of private property and just as determined to keep the dirty yokels out as he was to keep the Black creepy-crawlies out of his closed compound in suburban Cleveland.

To be sure, much of the prime recreation land is not necessarily farmland. The crisis of rural Canada is not only one of farmers—it is just that the farmers and their dependent farm towns are in the vanguard of it because they're feeling it most. If fishermen, for instance, are not feeling the brunt of the Trudeau depopulation policy, they are nevertheless not overjoyed at the idea of their shores becoming the property of strangers and being told to keep out. Examples are multiplying of fishermen suddenly cut off from access to their wharves—and other residents to their beaches—as ownership of the fields suddenly passes from a native who could not resist the money to the foreign bigwig who had the money.

Land grabs come under provincial rather than federal jurisdiction. But the prevailing comprador mentality that is permitting them is not one that stops at jurisdictions. It suffuses the entire Canadian power structure. American ownership is linked with 'development' and don't get uppity or you'll scare away investment. Far from trying to stop the lands sellout, most provincial governments are encouraging it.

The sudden value placed on rural lands has given added thrust to the apprehension of rural people and their determination to stand their ground against the Trudeau doctrine. So has the urban decay that has caused land values to rise. The reasons for not wanting to be 'retrained' by Canada Manpower for a position as welfare recipient in the urban slums are many times greater now that the cities' image is tarnished.

There is also the stigma attached to welfare that is one of the universal aspects of rural life. Although this attitude has often been interpreted as right-wing reactionism, it is a fact that to those whose lives are based on a rigorous minimum, a lack of the superfluities of materialism, welfare represents a breakdown in the human fabric. It has never been comprehensible to farmers that there should be a lack of work. They do not understand Liberalism. Rural poverty, if that's what it must be, to the rural person is still a cut or two above urban poverty. Besides, one fights better on one's own ground.

Beyond economics and politics, there is a cultural vengeance implied in the farmers' revolt. It is more than the anger of traditional communities being destroyed for nothing. It goes to the heart of what this country is all about.

Strongly rooted regional cultures are coming up hard against a colonial elite that has always taken American urban liberalism as its ideal. Toronto is the metropolis of English Canada: the great migrations of a century have fed into it—people bringing to it their particular ways from all parts of Canada, linking the metropolis to the outlying regions. Toronto has been the recipient of all the elements of a Canadian culture—but its elite has failed to recognize them as such. The outback, full of dull hicks, existed only in such measure as the CBC, the metropolitan dailies or the 'national' magazines recognized them. And the recognition was rather dubious: backward, ambitionless Maritimers, politically and psychologically perverted Québécois, vacuous red-necked Westerners.

The songs and stories of the great strikes, of the dead miners of Estevan and Glace Bay cut down by the bullets of provincial administrations, of the concentration camps of the Depression (indeed, of the Depression itself), of the wealth of other instances of common people fighting to assert their rights, not only remain untold and unsung, but the events themselves lie unrecorded in the official histories. Only Louis Riel (with qualifications) and the Eskimos have made it into the popular consciousness. But then the Eskimos and the Metis are no longer a threat. The Canadian Indians are still too dangerous to really make it, let alone the white working (and non-working) and rural class.

But the colonial elite has had second thoughts, now that its inspiration—US urban liberalism—has come to grief. And thus we are treated to the spectacle of this same elite overreacting in praise for every tidbit of Canadian culture, good or bad, running Pretty Pictures of Canada in *Maclean's*, 'discovering' Morley Callaghan—twenty years too late. And we are told that all of Canada is having an identity crisis vis-à-vis the US.

It is incredible that anyone could believe that the people who have tilled this land for three hundred years, whose fathers have spilled their blood and guts in the mines and on the railways, who are still deprived of rights on the fishing boats and are practically willing to starve (witness the Canso fishermen's strike) to acquire them, could have doubts about their sense of place or the value of their folkways in this country.

So there are not only farmers angry about their bread and butter, but a whole rural class whose way of life has been continually ridiculed by a pompous and hypocritical ersatz elite who had to borrow even their standards of ridicule, not to mention their standards of attainment.

The elements of a Canadian culture have always been present and will continue to be so. Perhaps we need a change of elite. Come to think of it, maybe we don't need an elite at all.

For Canada, ARDA was an avant-garde scheme, and still would be today were it re-introduced in original form, although much of what it proposed had actually been started in some Scandinavian countries a century before. Its inspiration was drawn largely from those countries where agriculture functioned efficiently and as a labour-intensive sector on a co-operative basis. In New Zealand, for instance, where techniques that are only trickling into Canada today were introduced twenty years ago, co-ops are so highly developed that in some instances they cover not only production, but every operation right through to the retail level is integrated into one co-operative structure.

The key is maximum development of renewable resources under a co-operative system. ARDA aimed at doing this, including development of forest co-operatives for marginal farmers, since a lot of poor farmers exist on the rim of forests where the land is not fertile; reforestation, water and soil conservation, fire roads; development of tourist and recreation facilities; fisheries; mining operations. All this was meant to allow the marginal farmer to pick up enough money here and there to free him from poverty.

Anyone familiar with Canadian politics should be able to guess what happened to such purity of purpose.

Instead of becoming a support system for marginal farmers, ARDA became a support system for bureaucrats and planners, and 'local participation' became parish pump politicos dishing out the new patronage bonanza.

The one area where ARDA seemed to be taking off for a while was the Bas du Fleuve (Lower St. Lawrence-Gaspé), where poverty is such that in some places entire towns go on welfare each winter. This was the plan's main pilot project, along with the Interlake district of Manitoba.

Entire communities showed up at public meetings to work out with the planners their dreams for local development. The Church, growing increasingly activist, participated. In fact there was so much *animation sociale* that some people in government started getting uneasy.

Since ARDA was channelled through the provinces (and Quebec was enthusiastic), the Bas du Fleuve scheme became known by the provincial name, BAEQ (for Bureau d'aménagement de l'est du Québec, or Eastern Quebec Development Bureau). In 1966 the long-awaited master plan was completed and dropped on Premier Daniel Johnson's desk. Nothing happened—a nothing compounded by the new Quebec-Ottawa jurisdictional disputes—and still nothing has happened. In the Bas du Fleuve, BAEQ has become synonymous with the most vicious bureaucratic fraud ever perpetrated on an underprivileged people. In the fall of 1970, a group of priests from the area signed a petition supporting the FLQ manifesto.

The grossest example of local politicians unable to resist temptation occurred in PEI, where big things were also in store. (Later, in 1969, an additional $17-million 'five-year plan' for the island was launched. The farmers' protest against corporate farming in 1971 indicates where this money has been going.)

Bulldozer owners on the northwest of the island discovered that all they had to do to get funds for 'ARDA ponds' (officially for fire and irrigation) was to say the word. So now the northwest tip is dotted with beautifully squared ARDA ponds, unrelated to any conceivable fire or irrigation. And there are the irrigation dams that had to be dug up again because no one checked to see what would happen upstream.

Then there's the greatest one of them all. It is said that on the west end of the island there's an airstrip built with ARDA funds that has a curved runway. Seems the contractor, in his haste to get the dough, hadn't checked out how much land was available. So why waste good asphalt? Just curve the end a bit. These new-fangled planes can do anything anyway.

ARDA continued to more or less dominate agricultural talk for a few years until the Liberal government, having returned to power in 1963, more or less forgot about agriculture amid the sound and fury of the Scandals and the lurchings of the Leaky Ship of State.

They had no reason to worry about it anyway. Was not ARDA—having become in Liberal hands a good instrument for regional 'cash infusions'—keeping snotty Eastern farmers happy? And were not the massive wheat sales to Russia and China (inaugurated under Hamilton) keeping snotty Western farmers happy?

But to the extent that anybody did worry about it, it seemed obvious that ARDA was going nowhere, especially since the Liberals weren't interested in making a Tory plan work anyway, and certainly not one with Commie tendencies.

Quietly, then, in 1964, came the first call for the government to move towards corporate agriculture: a report for the federal government by the Winnipeg consulting firm of Hedlin-Menzies suggested that 50 per cent of Eastern farmers get off the land and into other work. Get the poor farmers out and help the middle and rich ones, the report said.

Poor farmers were just a drain on the national economy. The report stated that its studies showed that half the farmers would get out of farming if other work were available. Many farmers would probably be willing to get into other work even now. But since there is no other work available, the question was and is academic. What is important is that farmers have since then made a psychological leap and now are committed to staying on the land. In fact Walter Miller, vice-president of the National Farmers' Union stationed at Guelph, says he knows of families that are scraping up odd jobs in local towns to support the family farm which is losing money.

From Hedlin-Menzies it was an easy step to the 1968 task force and the government's present commitment to corporate agriculture.

The operative word in Canada's free-market agriculture in 1971—as it has been for at least the last twenty years—is chaos.

For the multimillion-dollar food-processing, distributing and speculating industry, it can be described as 'profitable chaos'.

The key to the free-market system is that there are no controls on production. So farmers continually overproduce. When they have overproduced item A and sent prices for it crashing down, many of them will go to great expense to switch their production to whatever else is bringing in a good price, say item B. Within a few years, by the time all of them have switched, item B may be overproduced.

Overproduction means a continual supply of cheap food to ensure corporate profits. (Cheap food in no way means cheap food for the consumer.) Overproduction means a slow but sure death for the small farmer who cannot endure to produce at a loss as long as the corporate farmer can. Which means that agriculture—helped along nicely by governments in many little ways—keeps moving deliberately towards corporatism, centralism, destruction of rural lifestyles, etc. And corporatism in turn means even cheaper food—and without the chaos! (Let us genuflect before the genius of technocratic Liberalism.)

Whereas the big corporate farmer, often a speculator and distributor at the same time, can hold his products in storage until prices rise and he can dump, the small farmer cannot and takes the brunt of the loss of collective overproduction.

Then there's the cost-price squeeze. The farmer is hemmed in by spiralling costs on both sides. Studies for 1966 have shown that after the take of the 'upstream' (farm machinery, fertilizers, etc.) industries and 'downstream' (food processing, distribution) industries were deducted, less than 10 per cent of the retail price of food was returning to the farmer, a proportion which had declined steadily in the post-war period and was still declining. In many cases, even at face value of inflated dollars, the farmer is getting less today than he was twenty years ago.

On the one hand, the farmer is getting screwed by the multinational farm-machinery cartel (as was clearly shown by the Barber commission mentioned earlier). On the other, there are the vertically integrated food empires, against which the farmer must often not only compete but to whom he must sell and from whom he must buy in a system designed to ensure handsome profits at every level of the operation.

It must be noted that 'overproduction' is a relative term, and nowhere more than in Canada. Saddled with a dominant ruling party that was first indifferent to agriculture and now is downright hostile to it (now that it has discovered agribusiness), Canada has been steadily losing her share of export markets even as those markets grow by leaps and bounds. For instance, world wheat trade doubled between 1954 and 1968 but Canada's share of that market dwindled from 31 per cent to 21 per cent. Export markets for coarse grains doubled too, but Canada's share dropped from over eight per cent to less than three per cent.

And this is apart from the moral issue that is never far from the surface when discussing overproductive agriculture in the technological countries: why must wheat, or anything else, rot on the ground while millions are starving?

Chaos at the moment means this. Western farmers, stuck with massive surpluses of grain, have decided to use it to grow livestock. They have overproduced hogs, particularly, placing themselves and Eastern hog growers in trouble. Chickens and eggs have been massively overproduced, particularly in the East, precipitating 1971's curious 'chicken-and-egg war' with Quebec at the centre.

Quebec and the West are both special cases in agriculture, the very opposite of each other in outlook and approach but with their rural problems running parallel to the problems of their special collective identities.

The West, to its infinite credit, has never been amenable to the Liberal Party philosophy of keeping outlying regions quiet with 'cash infusions'. Given to forming radical political movements, the West's particular situation was too much for the Liberals to contain.

For one thing, a grains economy on a semi-arid plain is an extremely cyclical thing; and even if farmers' losses were fully covered it would still do little for the small-town businesses that exist only to service the farm industry. When farmers are having a bad year on the prairies the entire Western economy suffers, since there is little economic diversification. The giant food industries do nothing for the West, since produce is taken to Toronto or Montreal to be processed. Most of the Canadian farm community in fact is like that: a producer of raw materials for the economic centre of the country and a consumer of finished products—the same relationship that Canada as a whole has with the US.

Long-term total economic planning, coupled with a shift of power from the corporations to the farmers, is perhaps more urgently needed on the prairies than elsewhere in Canada. What the federal government has come up with instead is the Grains Stabilization Act, over which there has been a great furore in the House of Commons. Anticipating easy passage of the bill, the government proceeded to break its own laws by withholding payment of anywhere up to $92 million owed the farmers under existing wheat-storage legislation.

In terms of the real potential of the prairies—not only in local community and Canadian terms, but as one of the world's five great semi-arid plains—the difference, for the wheat farmer, between this act and the old system of government payments for storage of unsold wheat can be described as the difference between being shafted by a ten-foot pole and a twelve-foot pole.

The two extra feet are the extra thrust the Grains Stabilization Act has in hastening the demise of the small farmer. It will make payments to the wheat industry as a whole whenever total production falls below a set norm (the norm being average production over the last five years, itself a topic of bitter controversy since farmers say the last five were sub-average years). When the set amount is met by the industry as a whole, no payments will be made to anyone. In other words, the farmer who has a bad year while the industry as a whole exceeds the norm, gets nothing. What the government is saying to the farmers is, "Now you chickens get into that cage with the corporate wolves. We're going to have a little private enterprise here to see who comes out on top."

Quebec farmers are the poorest in the country. They are also the most passive. Associated generally with the Créditiste Party, they are one of the most conservative groups of people in Canada. They are the traditional colon-

Ralph Surette / 61

ized Québécois. (They contrast sharply with the forestry sector of semi-rural Quebec, where in a number of small towns entire populations have staged angry demonstrations against shutdowns of wood-cutting operations).

On the prairies the farmer membership has generally been more militant than its farm-union leaders. In Quebec the opposite is the case; the membership has to be prodded, since with its traditional reflexes it is easily frightened by the subtle threats of *la haute finance*, whereas farm leadership groups have acquired muscle as a spin-off of the nationalist movement.

However, the extreme conservatism of the colonized person is a curious phenomenon. There is a very thin line between that and desperation. Quebec's egg farmers, going under very quickly under a rising surplus on the Canadian market, had reached that point in 1966. They formed Fedco, the Quebec egg-marketing board, meant to set quotas for producers and act as the exclusive marketing agency for all eggs sold in Quebec. It also sets prices weekly.

This means that many corporate middlemen are eliminated. It also means that speculators can no longer dump surplus eggs on a captive Quebec market.

Poor Quebec farmers had long looked on with impotent rage as well-organized Ontario corporate farmers-cum-speculators not only undercut their livelihood, but often bought eggs from the US to dump on the Quebec market at cut-throat prices.

Since most of the poor farmers in the hassle were from Quebec and most of the speculators from Ontario—and with the usual paranoia that greets any move by Quebec—it came to be assumed across the land that Quebec was again trying to sabotage Confederation by unconstitutionally impinging on interprovincial trade, and that it was at 'war' with the other provinces, particularly Ontario, where broiler-chicken producers had set up their own marketing board several years before and were suddenly believed to have done it on the spur of the moment in 'retaliation' against Quebec, which has a surplus of broilers.

It was also a deliberate misconception that Fedco was trying to prevent eggs from coming in from other provinces. Quebec produces only about 50 per cent of its own consumption, and therefore necessarily had to import the rest from the other provinces.

The interprovincial aspect was largely a diversionary tactic by corporate farmers, and was settled with surprising ease when agriculture ministers from the ten provinces agreed in the summer of 1971 to set up their own egg-marketing boards and that the Canadian egg market would be shared according to mutual agreement. Manitoba, which had tried to block Fedco in the Supreme Court, agreed with the rest. It was a victory not only for Quebec egg farmers, but in the long run possibly for all Canadian egg farmers.

It must be stated categorically that Quebec farmers have nothing against English Canadian farmers, as demonstrated time and time again by their union, the UCC (Union catholique des cultivateurs, or Catholic Farmers' Union), which has passed countless resolutions over the years supporting the demands of Western wheat farmers. They know they have everything to gain by solidarity, and apparently the English Canadian farmers have realized it too in the egg question.

The 'unconstitutionality' of Fedco was not the real issue. It was just the best argument the food industry could come up with. One speculator said at one of the court cases that his opposition to Fedco was based on his belief in a "free Canada."

Fedco was more emphatically opposed, in fact, by the Quebec Food Council, representing the Quebec food industry, than by any province.

That is because the Quebec food industry is running scared these days. In recent controversy over a corporate increase in milk prices (Quebec is Canada's top dairy province, but its population—particularly in the Montreal slums—is the one that suffers most from lack of milk) there were calls by urban citizens' groups that milk become a public utility.

And there is a farm-union bill before a provincial legislative committee which the food industry fears will make the UCC the exclusive marketing agency for all agricultural products in Quebec, as Fedco now is for eggs. The Bourassa big-business government is permitting it, apparently sensing there are more votes to be gained that way, especially with the anti-big-business mood in Quebec.

The man behind the thrust of the Quebec farm movement is Albert Alain, president of the UCC. Although unknown in

English Canada since he speaks little English, he is probably second only to Roy Atkinson as the most important man in Canadian agriculture. It is through his efforts, his continual contacts with the grass roots, his computer grasp of the economics of agriculture, that Quebec agriculture is moving in the direction it is.

Although his approach is a soft-line diplomatic one, he is tough. "The food industry is scandalized that farmers want to control their production," he snapped with anger at one press conference. "But make no mistake. You don't see Noranda Mines, or anybody else in private business, fooling around with their production."

One more point must be mentioned about the troubles of Canadian agriculture. Research. Even the staid old Science Council of Canada this year rapped the federal government for lacking the kind of research that is necessary to get an export farm economy going.

It pointed out that since most of the corporations dealing in the agricultural sector are American owned, they spend little money on research in Canada. They spend it at home, naturally.

Most agricultural research over the past twenty years has been 'pure' research which has little to do with local conditions or the development of higher-yield native grasses, fruits, vegetables, livestock, etc. Research was dominated by the white-gloved technocrats—who in the early sixties had a regulation keeping farmers off federal agriculture-research stations because "it bothered the researchers."

There was always a minority group—the people associated with ARDA—who believed in applied research. But they never had the real power to change anything.

Had the Conservatives stayed in power after 1963, and Hamilton remained agriculture minister, the crisis in agriculture today would be with us anyway. The Diefenbaker Tories, although not as close as the Liberals to big business, were controlled by it nevertheless and sooner or later farmer power would have come in conflict with the slush fund.

ARDA now would be too late. Maybe it was too late in 1961.

The co-operative structures of the European and Pacific countries took a long time to build. In Canada, for many farmers the moment of truth is right now.

And agriculture, as a fundamental part of this country's society, not to mention the only way to live in dignity for thousands of people who have no other skills and will land in urban slums otherwise, will get nowhere as long as it is controlled by multinational corporations both 'upstream' and 'downstream'.

The problem for Canadian agriculture ultimately is the same that afflicts the rest of the economy—control by multinational corporations.

Perhaps the present rural unrest, coupled with unrest in the urban cores, will succeed at some point in electing some kind of government with the guts to start wresting Canada out of the control of the multinationals, including the farm machinery and food empires, and to return control of farming to where it belongs—to the hands of farmers.

Perhaps. Perhaps not.

Certainly the bursting forth of the radical, Saskatoon-based National Farmers' Union, which was formed only in 1969 and has grown very quickly since, indicates the extent of the discontent as well as its intensity.

Time is short.

Because if nothing happens, soon we can expect the biggest farmer of them all, the Bank of America, tired of whining Chicanos in the grape and lettuce fields, to cross the 'imaginary border' and gratefully accept from the Liberal Party a franchise to the entire prairies, as well as permission to divert the MacKenzie River to southern California and to sublet Saskatchewan to Howard Hughes for a private missile range.

Part Two
The Continentalist Pressure

The strongest pressure being applied to the Canadian economy is the continentalist pressure, the forces that are pushing Canada towards economic integration with the United States and establishing Canada's status as a permanent resource hinterland and consumer marketplace for the American economy.

The best way of grasping the magnitude of this pressure and of understanding what it really means for Canada is to look at some of the fields in which it is being exerted. That is what the chapters in this section do. They look in turn at oil, water, electronics, computers, military production and sport.

Canadians' awareness of foreign domination was generally restricted to the cultural fields till the turn of the decade, when the great Continental Energy Debate opened up. It had one healthy effect: people became aware of the peril in economic terms.

The realization that the United States was so hungry for Canada's oil and water that it was dropping customary diplomatic pretences was followed by an equally sobering discovery that the Liberal government was quite disposed to accommodate Washington.

The first piece in this section, "The Energy Con-Game," illustrates just what continental economics is and what consequences follow from it. It focuses on a turning-point in the continental energy debate: the famous Denver speech of then Energy Minister Joe Greene in May of 1970. The speech was widely hailed in the press as revealing a "courageous nationalist stance." It proved to be a thin veil of bravado disguising a policy that was anything but nationalist. And behind the brave words, there was developing a complicated struggle for control of the world's oil supplies that is far from finished today.

Related to the energy issue is the matter of our water resources. The second chapter is a brief examination of the

James Bay power development, in which Quebec is borrowing US money to generate hydroelectric power for sale mainly to US customers.

In 1971, the Ontario Federation of Labour published the findings of an investigation into a type of unemployment statistic not caused by temporary production cutbacks but by the wholesale closing of plants and industries. The title of the study was *Shutdown* and it pointed out that in one year, 1970-71, there were more factory shutdowns in Ontario than in any decade since 1930.

In an industry-by-industry survey, the study showed that some of the most advanced, indeed, many industries representing the 'technology of the future', were the most seriously affected by the factory closures. The Canadian electronics industry was a case in point.

The industry developed as a branch-plant operation, mainly, of American giants like General Electric and Westinghouse. The American giants, now euphemistically termed 'multinationals', either control outright or are involved in intricate partnerships and marketing-spheres arrangements with other foreign corporations. Thus decisions concerning the expansion or closing of given plants in Canada are determined by corporate needs which can have little or no bearing on the viability of any single plant. General Electric's Rexdale plant, the subject of the third piece in this section, was by any standard a modern, efficient operation. It was just, as they say, inconvenient. Or as one worker said as he explained the closure of his factory, "Somebody in a boardroom just pulled a pin from a map and we were gone."

What is true for industries like electronics holds in a slightly different way for the glamour field of computers. Because computer technology developed relatively recently, at a time when Canada was already well on the way to becoming a branch plant within the American sphere, there was little opportunity for any parallel development. But the growth of computer networks will affect not only the economic, but the entire social and cultural fabric of Canada. In terms of the twentieth century, the computer occupies the same position in the debate between east-west versus north-south continental development as did the railway.

The fourth chapter in this section, "Computers: Caught in the Continental Web," takes up a largely ignored warning issued in the summer of 1971 by the Science Council of Canada.

Continuing the theme of losing technological control because of foreign domination, we turn next to Canada's military-industrial sector.

Foreign domination doesn't necessarily mean foreign ownership, foreign domination can mean forcing one country's political priorities on to another's. And that's exactly what the case study of our defence industry illustrates.

In the first place, our military-industrial sector is so much an arm of the American defence-production industries as to be virtually indistinguishable from them. But it must be realized that military research and development (R & D) often sets the pace for new industrial development in many countries—and Canada is no exception. Since our military production is geared towards meeting Washington's needs, so is our R & D. And that means that industrial development in non-military areas is profoundly affected by the R&D we do to meet the specifications of the US defence establishment. If we develop a new kind of traction vehicle, for instance, it is likely to have been developed as a by-product of producing traction vehicles for American Arctic work.

The dilemma in this is obvious—who's setting our national goals in industrial research and development?

But industry and resources are not the only areas that have succumbed to foreign domination, as the last part of this section shows. It comes as no surprise to anyone any more that sport is big business. So why shouldn't it follow the logic of other business and move where the capital and the market are?

Officially Canada's national sport is lacrosse. This fact may provide some comfort as we watch hockey diluted and shipped south.

The Energy Con-Game
by Gordon Cleveland and *Last Post* staff

The 'Gee-Whiz' conference

If it's often proposed that it is a characteristic of the Canadian people to forgive, it is certainly a characteristic of the Canadian press to forget. It was certainly true May 12, 1970, at any rate, when our own Joe Greene, minister of Energy, Mines and Resources, flew back from Denver wrapped in a Canadian flag to be hailed by the attendant Toronto newspapers as one of our great nationalists.

What Mr. Greene had done to merit these accolades was to have told off the American oil barons, gathered for lunch in a Denver hotel, sternly warning them that Canadians were not to be toyed with. In fact, Canadians wanted no part of the American way of life, Mr. Greene declared, sending a wave of thrills through the Ottawa press gallery.

Like the grandiloquent speeches of presidents of Latin American republics before fruit-growers' associations in Washington, the Denver speech was clearly for domestic consumption.

Greene spoke before the Independent Petroleum Association of America, the surface organization of the massive southern oil lobby whose shadow cabinet is that large body of senators and congressmen that constitutes the front line of entrenchment in Washington.

Joe Greene was making a very calculated, if transparent, move.

It was the slightly pathetic move of pawn two squares forward in a continuing chess game Canada is going to lose—and which, it's not hard to argue, has already lost.

It revolves around an elusive political Snark labelled the 'continental energy policy', a major watershed in the waning of this country's political independence in the face of American economic imperatives.

*Published in the *Last Post*, April 1970.

For some time Canadian and American officials have discussed this scheme, which would lift all national barriers to the flow of Canadian oil, gas, water and coal to the increasingly thirsty markets of the northern industrial United States.

Since the beginning of the Nixon administration, increasing pressure has been brought on Ottawa to embark on the long negotiation road towards a North American free market in energy, which would open lucrative US markets to the Alberta oil and gas producers, but at a staggering political price.

It is a scheme that would set up a central authority on what resources would be exploited, how transported, to what markets, and at what prices. A sort of Common Market in oil, water and gas, it would mean that only the most profitable resources would be exploited, principally for the markets that need them most. It would constitute a suspension of national political considerations for economic expediency.

It would also mean plugging our energy production even further and irretrievably into the industrial needs of the United States, abdicating what tattered vestiges remain of an independent Canadian national resource policy.

The urgency with which Washington views the need to implement this continental scheme was reflected in the quota Nixon slapped on Canadian oil in March of 1970, a brisk reminder to Canada of its dependence on US oil markets and a move to pressure Ottawa into hastening its entry into such a continental policy.

What brought Joe Greene to Denver on May 12, then, was a lame opportunity to strengthen Canada's bargaining position through a little rhetorical coyness, to make squeaking-wheel noises in the face of Washington's crass behaviour and language during the continental energy debate and, more important, to stage Act One in the most remarkable piece of transvestism since Lot's wife: The Nationalization of J. J. Greene.

"The Canadian people," Greene thundered from his Denver podium, "will not tolerate decisions affecting Canadian security being made at the insistence of non-Canadians, even to win the prize of larger oil markets."

It is perhaps less than charitable to interrupt the cheers of "tough bargainer" and "outspoken nationalist" that greet statements like these, and to recall some of the inconsistencies that have accompanied the strangely shifting principles of our minister.

To begin, there was the delightful exercise in political amnesia which he foisted off on the public during a television hot-seat program on January 25, 1970. There he managed to declare that there's no such thing as a continental energy policy.

"No conversation I've ever had with the Americans included a continental energy policy as such," said Greene.

On April 23, in Washington, at the same press conference at which he announced that top-level discussions would begin in June on the sale of huge northern energy reserves, he did it again and declared firmly that "there's no such animal" as a continental energy policy.

These interesting "Continental-Energy-Policy?-I-Never-Heard-Of-It" cameos stemmed from his having been soundly spanked by the Liberal cabinet the previous December, for having shoved his foot in its collective mouth earlier that month in Washington.

For on December 4 of 1969, Joe Greene practically handed Canada's oil, gas and water to the US on a golden platter, in a remarkable press conference in the Canadian embassy that has since been nicknamed in Ottawa "The Gee-Whiz Conference."

Greene went to Washington, ostensibly to chat with US secretary of the Interior Walter Hickel about getting a bigger market for Alberta oil.

That seemed routine enough to the Canadian correspondents in Washington until Greene emerged from the meeting with Hickel into a press conference where he practically erased the 49th parallel.

Hickel had raised the continental energy-integration scheme with Greene during the meeting, and Greene could not contain his enthusiasm about the plan.

"He [Hickel] made this larger suggestion," Greene announced to the press, as if this was the first time he had heard of the scheme, "and speaking personally, the more I think and talk of the larger suggestion the more I thought, well, this is a great opportunity for Canada.

"This is his initiative, his leadership, that a broader approach be taken," he said. "I find this initiative of Secretary Hickel's extremely interesting."

Integrating the energy markets of the two countries would lead to the most economic utilization of these basic resources, he said. "The lower the energy costs are, the better off are Canadians. This is a great opportunity for Canada."

Asked whether this approach would lead to a substantial economic integration of the two countries, Greene replied: "Yes, I think it would."

Canadian economic interests must be considered first, he said, but if these jibe with the best interests of the United States then there would be no reason to be reluctant about integrating the markets because of narrow nationalistic impulses.

If Canada refused any economic integration with the United States for nationalistic reasons, he said, "It would be no more than a banana republic."

Then the crowning nationalist touch: It is "sufficient" for Canada to retain "political control," but "it is not important who gets the dividends, Wall Street or Bay Street." And Mr. Greene went on to develop a new refrain on the "undefended-border" theme and spoke in high praise of "the invisible border."

Back home in the banana republic, when the news reports made the papers and television, feathers started flying from every colouration of nationalist from Melville Watkins to John Diefenbaker. The Great Continental Energy Policy Debate was on without anybody much knowing what it was all about.

And back in Ottawa later, it must have taken Joe Greene every ounce of courage he ever had to steel himself and enter the room where the assembled Liberal cabinet was waiting to tear him to shreds.

Because the continental energy scheme was not, as Greene had implied in his December 4 press conference, something new that had just sprung out of Secretary Hickel's head on the spur of the moment. Nor was Greene totally ignorant of it before the meeting with Hickel. Only the Canadian public was ignorant.

And that was the measure of Greene's faux pas in Washington. Through his effervescent bungling, he had made what had been hitherto ignored by the press and unknown to the public, a major issue in the midst of a rising tide of nationalism and anti-American feeling in the country.

Actually the idea of the continental energy policy was not new. It has been occasionally mentioned before in Ottawa, and has been long mooted in the North American petroleum industry. Prime Minister Trudeau, when he visited President Nixon in Washington in late March of 1969, spoke favourably and hopefully about forming a continental energy policy. But this was mentioned in passing, and received scarcely any attention.

In fact, negotiations towards setting up such a continental plan had been going on between the two governments before Trudeau's visit.

But everything was being done quietly, outside the glare of national attention, without any suspicion on the public's part that one of the biggest economic deals ever considered by Canada and the United States was under negotiation.

Just a few dull tariff negotiations, with the odd little item appearing in the financial pages. Just some talks about a field of which most reporters understood little, and the public even less. Just something that, once consummated, would be hailed as a Liberal government victory in priming the oil and gas and hydro industries.

But Joe blew it.

Seven Sisters of Leviathan

As Washington reporter Jack Anderson noted in 1967: "The State Department has often taken its policies right out of the executive suites of the oil companies. When Big Oil can't get what it wants in foreign countries, the State Department tries to get it for them. In many countries, the American Embassies function virtually as branch offices for the oil combine . . ."

The naked political power of the oil combines has shown its hand clearly many times in recent world history. One might talk about how Iran, which tried in 1951 to nationalize its oil industry, was punished by an effective boycott of Iranian oil. The boycott launched a political crisis which ended in the deposition of Dr. Mossadegh's government in a coup directed and organized by the Central Intelligence Agency. The story ended happily for the US em-

pire—the British got back a fair percentage of their oil properties, American oil companies got a much larger share of
lands than previously, and the leading CIA representative in
the coup later became government-relations director for the
Gulf Oil Corporation in Washington.

The domination of the Western world over the Third
World, capped by the political and economic domination of
the United States over both and crowned by the domination
of corporate enterprise over the public interest is simply and
tersely set down in the political economy of resource exploitation—particularly energy and primarily oil.

And it is this:

The United States is the largest single consumer of
resources in the world.

Although it accounts for only 6 per cent of the world's
population, it consumes 35 to 50 per cent of the world's
mineral and energy resources depleted annually.

Narrowing further, the United States also has the world's
highest per capita energy consumption. By itself it uses 34
per cent of the world's energy.

This breaks down into these components:

    65% of the world's natural gas
    20% of its solid fuels (mostly coal)
    20% of its hydroelectric and nuclear electricity
    36% of its liquid fuels (mostly oils)

The United States is the largest and most important single
oil market in the world. Oil is the power base for the operation of the vast majority of its industrial enterprises.

The world oil market has historically been dominated and
controlled by the seven major internationally integrated oil
companies, commonly known as the 'International Majors'
or the 'Seven Sisters'.

In order of size based on sales, they are:

    Standard Oil of New Jersey
    Royal Dutch Shell
    Mobil
    Texas Oil (Texaco)
    Gulf Oil
    Standard Oil of California
    British Petroleum (BP)

With the exception of Shell, which is Dutch owned, and
BP, which is British owned and half government controlled,

the International Majors are US based, owned and controlled.

Sales of the five US majors in 1967 were $32 billion, or one-third of the gross national product of Canada.

This placed all five corporations among the top twelve industrial corporations in the United States.

Measured by profits, all five major oil companies were among the top seven industrial corporations in the United States.

In 1966, the US Majors' foreign investment represented 40 per cent of the total US direct investment overseas.

The five corporations had combined assets of about $40 billion, which is about one-fifth of the total assets owned by the one hundred largest US corporations.

In 1958, there were an estimated 190 US oil companies carrying on 598 separate operations in 91 countries.

In 1960 a Chase-Manhattan Bank study of the thirty-two principal oil companies in the US showed that they and their foreign operations produced over half (57.9 per cent) of all the crude oil in the non-Communist countries of the world. This included 62.9 per cent in the US, 56.3 per cent in the Middle East and 67.7 per cent in Canada.

In the most recent major study, in 1960, the Seven Sisters were shown to own over 70 per cent of all refining capacity in the non-Communist world.

This is the schema of the political economy of imperialism.

The international price structure

Essential to the domination of the International Majors is the maintenance of an artificially high world price structure for petroleum.

The Majors were able to sustain this artificial price-fixing structure because of their high vertical integration—that is, control over the exploration, the exploitation, the transport, the refining and a large part of the market (gas outlets, for example). In short, vertical monopoly.

World prices, including Canadian, have historically been set to a level required to make US oil production economic. Prices in Venezuela and the Middle East, for example, were set by the US Majors at a level high enough to guarantee profits for oil produced out of the 'Gulf of Mexico price zone', the Texas producing region.

Thus, even though companies like Jersey Standard and Gulf Oil in 1959 drew two-thirds of their net income from foreign operations, it was important to their profits to keep the Gulf of Mexico prices as high as possible. And since the cost of production in the Middle East is at most one-third of the cost of producing inside the US, it becomes crucial to the survival of the international cartels to maintain a high price level calibrated to the most expensive production area.

A task force set up last year by the Nixon administration reflected the magnitude of this price distortion. It revealed that if import restrictions into the US were lifted, and the country thrown open to the onslaught of cheap foreign-produced oil, the domestic wellhead price of $3.30 per barrel would decline by 1980 to $1.87 a barrel.

Thus Washington, sensitive to the lobbies of this emmensely powerful industrial sector, preserves the position of Texas oil from the competition of a cheaper external market, and delivers staggeringly inflated profits to the companies that explore in foreign countries.

The price-fixing knows no borders and extends directly into Canada. Here is an example of the operation of the price-control system in Canada in the late fifties:

The price of oil at the wellhead in western Canada in the late fifties varied between $2.50 and $2.65 a barrel. This price was set through a complicated procedure that assured that the price of western oil in central Canada would be the same as the price of oil from the closest major petroleum-producing centre in the US, in this case Illinois. This assured that Canadian oil could not compete effectively with the bulk of American oil, even in Canada's own markets.

This $2.50 to $2.65 a barrel from the West, according to the Borden Commission on Energy of 1959, actually cost only slightly in excess of one dollar (not including taxes) to produce. That is the measure of American control over the continental and world market price.

It might seem logical that one Canadian producer could rebel against these prices and cut his far below the American level, while still retaining a handsome profit over his production costs.

This does not happen because:

Sixty-two per cent of the Canadian oil industry is American controlled;

It is in the interests of the oil producers to maintain the highest possible price, therefore profit;

Any smaller Canadian producer who rebelled could easily be crushed in any price war; and

No one need worry about his price being undercut because imported oil from the international market is equally controlled.

As long as the companies play the game, they are prosperous and protected. If anyone tries to buck the game, he faces price wars, battles for markets and for supplies.

In this complex price-control system, coupled with the US control of Canadian oil production, already lies a continental energy policy.

But what the US wants extends even beyond this.

It's fair to begin to ask why our neighbour, who already sleeps with us when and if he chooses, is suddenly proposing marriage. And why Joe Greene ran to Washington lifting the Liberal Government's skirt.

Oil and empire

The symbol of the S.S. Manhattan is the Esso tiger with earmuffs, grinning on the background of the US and Canadian flags and representing the remarkable adaptability of American capital when in crisis. But a more imposing symbol is the S.S. Manhattan itself. Because it is clearly and simply the physical incarnation of the desperate hunt for cheap North American oil that the US Majors have launched in a bid to scrape out of their squeeze.

The entire project is a $40-million oil venture sponsored jointly by Humble Oil (a division of Standard Oil of New Jersey), Atlantic Richfield and British Petroleum.

It was a rush job.

The 115,000-ton tanker, the largest merchant vessel sailing under the US flag, combining more steel and power than many of the new supertankers, had to be prepared in such a hurry that she was split into four sections and sent to shipyards from Maine to Alabama in order to strengthen and convert her for her unique icebreaking voyage through the Northwest Passage to Prudhoe Bay, Alaska.

For part of the escape that the US oil producers see from their squeeze lies in Alaskan oil. And the S.S. Manhattan is the measure of their hurry. So much in a hurry that they took their chances with a sensitive Canadian public worried about sovereignty.

For the last couple of years, the companies have scrambled for offshore oil, drilling off the east and west coast. This frantic search led to massive pollution of the California beaches. On the east coast a simmering territorial dispute with Canada bubbled into the headlines. But with all this, the offshore oil scramble proved a failure.

The hope for cheaper oil for the northeastern market has now turned to Alaska—but the problems of transportation are immense.

Three alternatives are being considered: one is giant tanker transport, which is the basis of the Manhattan test voyages: this may prove uneconomical and slow because of heavy pack ice. The second is already being readied: a $900-million trans-Alaska pipeline from the giant Prudhoe Bay discovery of 1968 to Valdez in southern Alaska. The third is a pipeline from Alaska through Canada down to the northeastern markets—but it would be difficult to negotiate such a pipeline outside of a continental energy policy.

But even Alaskan oil, if all the problems are overcome, is at best only a short-term solution, and only part of a larger solution that has been under negotiation for almost a year.

Two weeks before Alaska oil was discovered in July of 1968, the Department of the Interior warned in a survey that the discovery rate in the United States was insufficient to meet continuing demands. For the first time it was publicly admitted that there was a supply crisis looming, and this had its effect on the oil industry and the government in their search for solutions.

Obviously, the discovery of oil reserves in Alaska two weeks later was a lucky reprieve. But that only postpones the problem—current estimates of the Alaska reserves are 10 million barrels in the Prudhoe pools, and that would only be about two years' supply for the US.

The Canadian National Energy Board has estimated that the US would have, by 1975, an oil deficiency of .6 to 1.8 million barrels a day—this is even calculating the Alaska reserves. However, in 1990, this deficiency will have increased to 7.4 to 9.5 million barrels per day. So in the short run, until 1975 and perhaps 1980, the demand for oil will not be overwhelming. The US can get along with its own, Canadian, and some overseas imports, especially if they succeed in finding some more domestic supplies.

But by 1990 those deficiencies will be so monumental, Canada could not even supply the deficiencies herself.

And so the US government is engaged in the building of a restructured world energy policy, balancing political and economic and military considerations to ensure a secure future supply of energy.

The mechanism that will make us a link in that policy, the moves of the oil Majors in concert with the US and Canadian governments, are already well advanced.

Step one to the solution of the US oil industry's woes is exploitation of Alaskan oil. Step two is a continental energy policy with Canada.

In late March of 1969, while Canada's prime minister was paying his first official visit to the US capital, a high-level committee, comprising some of the most important members of the Nixon cabinet, was established to study the reform of the crumbling national oil policy. Part of its task was to find some answers to the looming depletion of US resources.

The calibre of the men assigned to this task force reflected the concern of the Nixon Administration: Shultz, the secretary of Labor who chaired the committee and whence the report got its name; Rogers, secretary of state; Kennedy, secretary of the Treasury; Laird, secretary of Defense; Hickel, secretary of the Interior; Stans, secretary of Commerce; and Lincoln, director of the Office of Emergency Preparedness.

The Shultz committee released 393 pages of texts, diagrams and statistics in a cold, calculated look at import policies and alternative sources of supply, and weighed them all in terms of the national interests and security of the United States.

The committee split essentially over replacing the present system with tariffs or keeping the present system of quotas with some minor changes. The majority of the committee chose the first alternative; a minority composed of Hickel and Stans chose the latter.

But both sides basically agreed on one thing—that the needs and security of the United States required the negotiation of a continental energy policy with Canada as soon as possible, as an important supplemental source of supply for the United States.

Quite clearly the US sees political factors and trade relations closely interlocking. The Americans are likewise clear in their own minds that there is going to have to be a further political integration involved in increased imports of Canadian oil, rather than a simple technical and economic change.

The majority report states: "In our judgment, Canadian and Mexican oil is nearly as secure militarily as our own, although complete realization of these security benefits will require fully understood and harmonized energy policies."

It will require more than that. It will require Ottawa agreeing to place the needs of the United States over the needs of eastern Canada in any petroleums-supply emergency.

The minority report states: "Canada is generally considered to be a secure source of oil for the United States in an emergency, except to the extent that eastern provinces are dependent on eastern-hemisphere oil."

And Greene is promising the Americans that if the Middle East blockades North America, Canada will bind itself to provide its oil to the American market, even though that blockade would mean all Quebec and Maritime industry stagnating for lack of the same Middle Eastern oil.

The criteria by which the US chooses to offer its matrimonial bonds to us are never stated more clearly than in these two quotes from the Shultz report:

"The pre-eminent position of the United States in the world depends in large part on the uninterrupted flow of oil and its products to its armed forces and civilian economy."

And it proceeds to note the contingencies:

"We begin by noting the major difficulties that might attend dependence on foreign supplies:

1) War might possibly increase our petroleum requirements beyond the ability or willingness of foreign resources to supply us;

2) In a prolonged conventional war the enemy might sink the tankers needed to import oil or to carry it to market from domestic production sources such as Alaska;

3) Local or regional revolution, hostility or guerrilla activities might physically interrupt foreign production or transportation;

4) Exporting countries may be taken over by radical

governments unwilling to do business with our allies;

5) Communist countries might induce export countries to deny their oil to the West;

6) A group of exporting countries might act in concert to deny their oil to us, as occurred briefly in the wake of the 1967 Arab-Israeli War;

7) Exporting countries might take over the assets of American or European companies;

8) Exporting countries might form an effective cartel raising oil prices substantially."

And so the Shultz report outlines the probable guaranteed sources of supply and urges the administration to lock them into energy-satellite status:

"The United States should work diligently with Canada to reach a continental energy policy that assures our mutual security. Such a policy should cover energy broadly, and should deal with not only oil but natural gas, coal and hydroelectric and nuclear sources. Pending agreement on such a policy, which may take several years to negotiate, Canada and the United States should develop an effective mechanism to permit an orderly growth of imports of oil and natural gas from Canada."

To hear Mr. Greene talk, the US is offering us this because we've been nice guys, and this "great opportunity for Canada" is completely separate from political considerations. Oh, it might lead to some substantial integration of economies but, as we know, it doesn't matter where the profits really go—either Wall or Bay Streets.

"Advance with trumpets . . ."

There was something pathetic about Joe Greene thumping a nationalist fist before the oil men in Denver, warning them that Canada will not stand for this or sit idly by for that. Only Canadians might have really believed what he said, and the hollow posture he assumed, because they would like to believe what he said is possible. But the men he spoke to in Denver must have viewed the performance with amusement.

The fundamental choices were made years ago, when we geared our resource policy to the United States' needs, when we set no national goals on energy exploitation; and even farther back, when we decided it didn't matter where it all went, Wall Street or Bay Street.

We have been locked into American market and security requirements throughout our entire history as a major exporter.

Canada's first mass oil export was born of California's energy shortage in the time of the Korean War. The basis of the co-operation was, from the beginning, not economics, but political and military security. The initiative was American, not Canadian.

The United States Petroleum Administration for Defense decided in 1951 that California needed more oil, the West's traditional oil shortage having been aggravated by the war. A safe source of oil was required; for strategic reasons Canada was chosen to be the supplier.

A pipeline from Alberta to California was constructed, and a $65-million tab was picked up mostly by the major American oil companies.

The framework for this first exercise in continental energy planning had been set out in a joint agreement in 1950, which in effect established a sort of economic NATO or NORAD for scarce resources in time of emergency. It gives us a view of what a continental energy policy would be. That agreement declared that the two governments agree to "co-operate in all respects practicable . . . to the end that the economic efforts of the two countries be co-ordinated for the common defense, and that the production and resources of the two countries be used for the best combined results . . ."

What the US wants now is a more explicit agreement making an integrated economic market in resources permanent.

Canada decided in its oil policy of the early 1960s not to form its own national goals and markets but to be a supplemental supplier to the more lucrative US markets.

The interim compromise of the early 1960s saw Canada split into two markets along the Ottawa Valley—Alberta produced for the US, while the East was left to foreign imports. It's that compromise that is now cracking under the weight of the international shifts in the market, and the tensions within the US.

Canada did not opt then for a national energy system because of the very structure and development of the oil industry in this country.

Seventy-four per cent of Canada's petroleum and natural

gas industry is foreign-owned. Of that, 54 per cent is American, but actually 62 per cent of the industry is under American control.

Percentages are only half the picture. Concentration of ownership is equally important.

A 1964 study showed that petroleum and coal products in Canada created $2460 million in sales.

Ninety-nine per cent of these sales were made by the twenty largest firms.

Of these twenty firms, eighteen are foreign controlled.

Since Alberta, in 1968, produced 68 per cent of the total Canadian output of crude oil (Saskatchewan produced 24 per cent), we are speaking basically of Alberta oil. Almost half of Alberta's annual provincial income stems directly from the oil industry.

Canadian oil is too expensive to sell abroad—almost three times more expensive than Middle East oil. So we have a commodity that is unmarketable overseas. But we allowed it to be developed, and we allowed a sector of our economy and our country to become dependent on it.

If our American markets are lost, a massive recession will hit the West. Our economy, then, is controlled by the economic vicissitudes and political decisions of a foreign country.

The American offer today is a simple exchange—yield what political control you have over your energy production, provide for our needs and reap the economic benefits. Don't, and reap the economic consequences.

It is uneconomic for Canada to have become the ninth largest oil producer in the world. Our oil is only marketable in one market, because of the high fixed and controlled prices.

All these decisions have been made for us—by the US oil companies that determined we shall become a major oil producer; by the US oil companies that control the continental price structure we are locked into; and by the US government that has carte-blanche to blackmail us by simply not buying.

If this is not a continental energy system, then it's the next best thing.

That system is speedily disintegrating, causing massive pressure on the Canadian oil industry.

Canadian producers are getting steadily frozen out of the American market because of such developments as Alaska oil finds, and the building of a pipeline to Illinois that speeds Texas oil to the northeastern US industries. The Ottawa Valley line has already begun to crumble, and the big Ontario market has begun to fall to foreign oil.

In the short run, the US can dry up the Canadian oil industry without suffering any setbacks. But in the longer run, we will be a crucial supplementary source of supply. The long-run thirst that will develop in the US explains Washington's push for the continental policy. The short-run security of the US market is the club with which it can clout us into that continental scheme.

And these are the choices we have allowed ourselves to be faced with:

Agree to a continental-energy scheme and pay the political price of taking a giant step towards further economic and political domination by the United States; Face the fact that our oil is uneconomic and get out of the oil business, causing a massive recession in the West; Or make the decision we refused to make over ten years ago (under pressure from the US Majors) and build the Alberta to Montreal pipeline.

The last choice may end up being the least of three evils, but it's no easy way out.

It would mean that we would make ourselves a self-contained market, consuming in the East the surplus that is produced in the West. And we would have to pay the price in dollars, because that oil will be even more expensive in the East than current price levels on the imported oil. We would, in effect, be publicly subsidizing an industry that has grown out of proportion to our national needs—paying the price of the decisions of the US oil companies.

The quandary we face on the oil question aptly represents the economic crisis in the country.

To control the development and flow of an industrial sector such as oil, there is virtually no step that can be taken, short of nationalizing exploitation and processing.

Failing that, the government has no alternative but to get 'the best possible deal' from Washington. Or put more realistically, Ottawa can only negotiate the terms of surrender.

Since negotiating surrenders, economic or otherwise, is a nasty business to conduct before the public, Ottawa naturally tries two contradictory tacks:

First, it pretends the problem does not exist, or at least is highly exaggerated.

Second, it creates a nationalist smokescreen to blur the fact that what is taking place is not exactly something to stir the patriotic heart.

When surrendering, wear your best uniform and all your medals. Or, as a British trade unionist once said about how to conduct yourself in a rout: "Advance with trumpets, retreat with cymbals."

When Joe Greene so preciously remarked in the middle of it all that the Liberal Party has to assume the position of nationalist spokesman lest legitimate nationalist demands take on a socialist flavour, he summarized it all for years to come.

Water: The James Bay Deal
by Jim Littleton

On April 30, 1971, Premier Robert Bourassa of Quebec announced to a crowd of 5,000 Liberal Party enthusiasts gathered in the Quebec City sports coliseum that his government was about to launch the biggest industrial project in the history of the province. The development would involve harnessing five of the main Quebec rivers flowing into James Bay; it could have an ultimate generating capacity of about 10.6 million kilowatts and an annual production of more than 70 billion kilowatt-hours, at a cost of approximately $6 billion. These figures are provided by Hydro-Quebec, and would seem to be accurate.

Somewhat less certain was Premier Bourassa's claim that the project would provide 125,000 jobs, including 3500 almost immediately. Even less clear were the questions of how the electricity would be marketed and where the $6 billion would come from.

The scope of the project is certainly impressive. The plan contemplates diverting the Nottaway River into the Broadback by way of a canal twenty-two miles in length, and then channelling the combined flow into the Rupert River through three large parallel tunnels, each three-quarters of a mile long. These water-diversions would require the construction of about 120 dikes ranging up to 100 feet in height and totalling approximately 60 miles in length. To the north, the Eastmain and La Grande Rivers would be harnessed to provide additional energy.

Because the estuary of the Rupert River is 475 miles distant from Montreal, the Eastmain 525 and the La Grande 625 miles away, the power would have to be conducted over extra-high-voltage transmission lines, at least on the order of magnitude of the 735,000-volt lines already in use in other parts of Quebec. These lines were originally the highest voltage and the largest capacity power lines in the world. The

*Published in the *Last Post*, September 1971.

complex would be by far the largest in Canada, having the equivalent of a quarter of Canada's present total generating capacity.

The idea of developing the hydroelectric potential of the James Bay area is not new. The matter had been under study for several years by Hydro-Quebec officials and in 1967 the late Premier Daniel Johnson had urged them to accelerate their review of its possibilities. In the months immediately preceding his announcement of the project, Bourassa had made a series of junkets to American and European money capitals in search of investment funds for Quebec. The Montreal press had reported enthusiastically on his good relations with several US financiers, particularly David Rockefeller of the Chase-Manhattan Bank. Immediately after the project was announced, the premier attempted to dispel any misunderstanding that might arise as to the source of funds when, on May 3, he told a Montreal meeting of the Canada Manufacturers' Association that "The money will come from where the money is—and you know where the money is."

It can be assumed that anyone who is on a first-name basis with the Rockefellers indeed knows where the money is. Others were not so sure, and one Quebec City newspaper, *l'Action*, even ran a headline to the effect that the US government-controlled Tennessee Valley Authority would invest one and one-half billion dollars in James Bay development. However, by July, American business leaders themselves were making serious statements about James Bay. Donald S. MacNaughton, chairman and chief executive officer of the Prudential Insurance Company of America, said in Montreal that his firm, which according to him already has 1.8 billion dollars invested in Canada, would eventually invest $125 million in the project. "I can't conceive of us doing less than that for a project that size," he said. His attitude was summed up in his comments on the Churchill Falls hydro project in Labrador, in which Prudential also has invested $125 million, when he said that it was "a splendid example of what American capital can do."

Along with talk about where the money would come from, there was also speculation as to where the power would go. Electrical-power shortages, 'brown-outs' and attendant problems have already reached awesome proportions in the northeastern United States. The current slogan of the Consolidated Edison Company in New York is "please save a watt." Estimates in the US put the cost of additional power generated by thermal or nuclear plants at approximately ten mills or one cent per kilowatt-hour. It is calculated that James Bay power can be delivered for seven to eight mills per kilowatt-hour. In comparison, power from Quebec's Manicouagan hydro complex is delivered in Montreal for four mills per kwh. It is reasoned that although the power will be expensive by Quebec standards, energy generated at James Bay will be competitive on the US market.

The assumption in respect to the American market is that the generating capacity of James Bay will be surplus to the needs of Quebec. For example, the *Montreal Gazette* in a feature article dated May 4, 1971, stated that for the success of the project, Bourassa "must be assured of clients in the United States since the James Bay project is so big it will produce more hydro power than Quebec will need in this century." The implication clearly is that American capitalists will invest in a project whose output is desperately needed to meet the energy requirements of the US industrial heartland.

The fallacy in this is to assume that the output of James Bay would be surplus to the needs of Quebec. The present total output of Hydro-Quebec is 10,738,000 kilowatts, with a surplus of 108,000 kilowatts. Hydro-Quebec projects that by 1980 its total capacity, including the output of programs currently under study, will be doubled at 21,446,000 kilowatts, but that there will be a *deficit* in terms of Quebec demands of 4,621,000 kilowatts. By 1984 it is anticipated that the total energy available will be 29,258,000 kilowatts with a deficit of 12,433,000 kilowatts. It is obvious that there is a serious conflict between Quebec's own requirements and the needs of the energy-starved United States.

At present, the only direct customer that Hydro-Quebec has in the United States is the Vermont Electric-Cooperative which has a total of 539 customers in three small border communities. During the peak summer period a relatively small amount of energy is supplied to the Consolidated Edison Company of New York City through the systems of Long Sault, Inc., and the Niagara Mohawk Power Corporation. During three months in the summer of 1970 this was at the rate of 94,000 kilowatts. In addition, long-term agreements for the supply of energy are in force with

Ontario Hydro and the New Brunswick Electric Power Commission. High-voltage transmission lines to the United States do not yet exist.

Hydro-Quebec was originally formed in Montreal in 1944 when a local, privately owned utility was expropriated. In 1963, under the leadership of René Lévesque as Liberal minister of Natural Resources, Hydro-Quebec expanded rapidly by acquiring the shares of eight privately owned companies in various parts of the province. In the words of the official *Story of Hydro-Quebec*, "although the takeover is often referred to as nationalization, what actually transpired is a far cry from the visions which this term usually conjures up. The takeover was a government decision and Hydro-Quebec, in carrying it out, tried to be as fair as possible to all parties concerned. A committee consisting of representatives of Hydro-Quebec, the government and the financial community was appointed to study the matter and, following the committee's recommendations, Hydro-Quebec made offers which the shareholders of the various companies agreed to accept."

It is clear that Hydro-Quebec is not in any sense a socialist institution, but an example of an efficiently run state-capitalist enterprise, and that the role it plays in the James Bay project will have little social consequence. Yet the controversy in the debate in the Quebec National Assembly on Bill 50, which was eventually passed as the James Bay Region Development Act, centred on precisely that question.

The principal object of the bill is to incorporate the James Bay Development Corporation, whose purpose will be to develop the natural resources in the area. Hydro-Quebec and the new corporation share a subsidiary which is to act in the development of hydroelectric resources in the area. In addition, other subsidiaries are set up to develop other resources. The debate centred on the opposition contention that Hydro-Quebec itself could adequately handle the James Bay development, as its successful record with the massive Manicouagan project demonstrated. The points that the Development Corporation would be open to patronage and politicking, and that its board would hold virtual dictatorial powers over an area one-sixth the territory of Quebec were forcefully made throughout the deliberations. During second reading the debate became so heated that violence erupted twice on the floor of the National Assembly and the official record did not print all of the calumnies that were hurled back and forth. Despite the attempts at filibustering by the opposition, the bill was passed after nine days of debate on July 14, 1971, by a vote of 73-6.

During most of the tempestuous nine days, as in most discussion of the James Bay project, scant attention was paid to the real ways in which it would work against the interests of the people of Quebec. Bourassa's claim that it would provide 125,000 jobs hardly stands up to scrutiny. The Churchill Falls hydro development in Labrador, costing approximately one billion dollars, employed 6300 workers at its peak construction period in the summer of 1970. When it is in full operation, it will create perhaps 150 permanent jobs. It is difficult to see how a project utilizing six times as much capital can create twenty times as many construction jobs. The question of what would happen to workers temporarily employed in construction after the project is completed was left entirely unanswered.

The fact is that hydroelectric development, like all resource-extractive industries, is highly capital-intensive in the long run. To supply energy for manufacturing industries in the United States, it consumes enormous amounts of capital investment and does not create any substantial increase in permanent employment in the area where it is located. This effect is further emphasized if by supplying relatively cheap power to the eastern United States, it makes the secondary industries, which are located there and are relatively labour-intensive, more efficient and consequently more competitive. Finally, the massive influx of American capital which is anticipated by Premier Bourassa can only serve to complete the dependency of the Quebec economy on that of the United States, and make it more vulnerable to the instability that the US economy is now experiencing.

When US investors have control of so massive a piece of the economy as that contemplated in the James Bay project, it is certain that they will exert every pressure imaginable to maintain the social and political status quo in Quebec. This, of course, is perfectly consistent with Robert Bourassa's political aims.

Whether Pierre Trudeau and Richard Nixon ever sit down

and formally sign a document entitled "The Continental Energy Deal" or not, the fact remains that the basic provisions of such a contract have been and are in the process of being worked out. Among the components of the deal, one of the most important certainly is the vast reserve of hydroelectric energy in Quebec.

Electronics: The Sad Saga of 15KY8A
by Rae Murphy

Strange as it may seem, while the Canadian market for television and other products of the electronics industry remains strong—Canadians bought 400,000 colour TV sets in 1970—the Canadian electronics industry is fast going the way of the buffalo and the whooping crane.

The whole sad story can perhaps be summed up in the name of one of those little tubes that twinkle in the back of everyone's television set. 15KY8A is a 'bread and butter' tube—two, three, sometimes four of them are designed into every set. Up until three years ago they were all stamped— "Made in Canada." Now they are all stamped—"Packaged in Canada."

And thereby hangs a tale.

Sometime in late 1970, an unsung hero of our consumer society flicked a switch and became the one millionth Canadian to receive the world of television in living colour.

Colour television, from a sales if not an aesthetic point of view, has become an unqualified success in Canada. Transmission began on an experimental basis only five years ago. As recently as 1968, a mere four per cent of the market was represented by colour sales. Yet by the end of 1970, when Mister Million bought his, 20 per cent of all television sets sold in Canada were colour. Moreover, the Electronic Industries Association claims that "the dramatic upsurge during this [two-year] period in colour TV sales—especially in the popular large-screen sizes—has been developed primarily by Canadian-designed and manufactured units."

Great news, it would seem, for the Canadian electronics industry, and if one is interested in the fortunes of one particular manufacturer—Canadian General Electric—the spirit is strictly gung-ho.

GE's employee magazine *Progress* quoted the "fighting

*Published in the *Last Post*, January 1971.

words" of its general manager, Jack Pollock: "We are definitely in the home-entertainment business and intend to stay in the home-entertainment business. Furthermore, we have aggressive plans for increasing our share of the market and building a bigger business."

"A lot of guys were pissed off when they read that in the company's magazine," says Neil Young, a leader of the union representing the workers at General Electric in Toronto. Small wonder. For they had recently been told by the company that when the old year was finished, they were finished too. As of January 1, 1971, the company was abandoning colour picture-tube production in Canada and its Rexdale plant was going to be turned into a warehouse.

No one, of course, has any doubts that General Electric is going to remain in the "home-entertainment business," but it is becoming increasingly likely that its branch plants in Canada will be going out of business. The closure of the Rexdale plant—which originally produced black and white picture tubes and recently switched to colour tubes—is the latest example of production cutbacks and plant closures that have brought employment at General Electric and Westinghouse to approximately half of what it was in 1969.

In 1970, domestic production of electronic tubes was 9.5 million units and imports numbered 14.1 million units. In 1965 domestic production was 15.2 million units and imports were 11.1 million. Since 1965, Canadian production has dropped 5.7 million and imports have jumped by 3 million.

The story was told quite graphically by the Electronics Industries Association in a brief to the federal government in 1970. According to the EIA, in 1963 more than 61 per cent of the entertainment-receiving tubes sold in Canada were domestic and 1427 people were directly employed in their manufacture. By 1970, 31 per cent of the market was domestic and 435 people were directly employed. By the end of 1971, they estimated, about 25 per cent of the market would be handled at home, giving employment to only 200 workers.

One of the problems with the abstract world of statistics and percentage points is that it often obscures the real world, and the lives of men and women who have to make their way in it. The difference between 1427 jobs and 200 involves the plight of workers, many of them highly skilled and with years of experience. The majority of the workers affected by the cutbacks at General Electric in Toronto have between fifteen and forty years seniority; suddenly they are without work and without a 'marketable skill'.

Government and industry spokesmen generally explain layoffs in the industry by talking of 'technological change', and there is no doubt that electronic tubes are becoming obsolescent. However the decline in the use of electronic tubes has not been all that rapid, and even industry spokesmen state that tube production, given tariff protection, could remain economically viable for up to ten more years. Yet, as an 'anti-inflationary measure', the federal government telescoped the Kennedy Round tariff-agreement reductions and dropped the tariff on imports three percentage points in one year, rather than over the originally scheduled three years. In the meantime, the United States increased its own tariffs.

An article in the *Financial Post* in June 1969 announced: "Electronics industry will adopt more mature outlook." This "mature outlook" involved mainly mergers and concentration of production. "Gone are the days," the article stated, "when it [the electronics industry] relied basically on the manufacture of radio and television as its main props. With the thrust into space communications, data-processing equipment, automation, flight simulators and integrated components—to name but a few of its newer products—the industry must restructure itself to become economically viable and more proficient. Otherwise there is a danger of the industry's position in the economy fading."

It was expected by the author of the article that the "more mature outlook" would involve a number of mergers and "there may be some interesting takeover bids and a tendency to agglomerization."

The in word now is 'rationalization'—the pooling of production facilities and increasing specialization. However, this has been going on in the industry for a number of years. For example, the late General Electric Rexdale plant was a runaway plant that used to be called Radio Valve Company, producing tubes for a number of manufacturers. It didn't run away too far—from southern Toronto to the north end of Metro to avoid unionization—but in the process of its reorganization, Radio Valve Ltd. became the exclusive property of Canadian General Electric.

As this shows, the Canadian television and radio manufacturing industry was always highly rationalized—tubes and component parts are, for the most part, quite interchangeable and the really distinctive feature of most makes is the trademark.

Rationalization has a nice progressive ring to it, and conjures up visions of efficiency and business-like dispatch. But it did not save television manufacture in Canada, and in the context of our economic relationship to the United States it simply means that instead of many branch plants we will have few. The Canadian section of the industry will specialize in the manufacture of certain components—until these components either become obsolete or can be produced with greater economy in some other part of the American Empire. Then they will be phased out of business just like the electronic tube.

Such decisions about obsolescence and efficiency are not made in Canada. And there can be quite a distinction between the elements that determine what is efficient from the national interest of a given country, and what is efficient from the viewpoint of a 'multinational'—but Yankee to the core—corporation.

The *Financial Post* noted the disturbing fact that Canada imported more than $440 million worth of electronic equipment in 1967, and declared that: "...the industry is feverishly trying to get more co-operation among its own members to co-ordinate... the various and complex requirements of the front-end manufacturers. In this way, more economy could be effected by higher volume purchases even manufacture..."

The Canadian electronics industry has developed as a branch plant of the American parent and has never been completely self-sufficient. The rationale was stated by an official of CGE: "It is important to realize that the importation of tubes into Canada is, and always has been, necessary. This is because Canadian manufacturers only produce those types which present enough volume to make production in Canada economically viable. Historically, about 250 types are made in Canada, while our price list contains 2000 types. The difference is represented by all the types used in relatively small quantities and imported, mainly, from the USA."

The author of this company memo goes on to discuss the general problems of the electronic-tube market and ends with this forecast: "In this free-trade environment, the basic manufacturing of goods will move to the location in the world where the particular commodity can be produced most efficiently. The rate at which this happens can only be influenced by the short-term attitude of the governments involved and the utilization of controls like tariffs, non-tariff barriers, quotas, subsidies, etc. The current attitude of the federal government in Canada does not reflect any particular concern for the electronic-component industry."

If it was only the problem of electronic tubes for the "home-entertainment business," even this would be serious enough. But in fact this is only the symptom, and judging by the noises emanating from the industry, the writing is on the wall for all its branches.

Now, spokesmen for the troubled industry have found a new scapegoat to blame for the troubles at home—the Japanese.

In the fall of 1970, Léon Balcer, president of the Electronics Industry Association (and former Conservative cabinet minister), read in the *Canada Gazette* that the government would investigate allegations that TV sets from Japan are being dumped on the Canadian market. "We are gratified," said Mr. Balcer. "It is a very encouraging initiative."

The EIA has been after the government concerning Japanese imports into Canada, and throughout the industry the battle of the briefs has been joined. Statistics roll from the papers of researchmen and economists, while the PR men issue thunderous Churchillian statements about fighting foreign competition, cost and quality control, and maintaining jobs for the good, sober, Canadian working class.

An example of this appeared in the *Toronto Star* of August 15, 1969, which headlined an article on the electronics industry: "Canadian radio-TV tube makers begin hitting back at imports." The article noted that 75 per cent of the market is now captured by foreign imports and said: "Although the bulk of the imports are from the United States, sold by Canadian General Electric and other US subsidiaries, Japanese tubes are causing the real concern."

Why are they so mad at the Japanese?

Because, says Jim Smart of CGE, "the Japanese have concentrated on tube types made in Canada and they are 20 per cent cheaper."

The fact that Japanese tubes are cheaper doesn't affect the Canadian customer in the least, as the EIA points out: "The Canadian consumer does not benefit from the low-cost Japanese imports since extra margins go only to service dealers who supply the consumer at Canadian-made list prices."

Cheaper Japanese prices may not mean anything to the consumer but there is plenty of money in them for the wholesaler. Both Westinghouse and General Electric, after a ritualistic protest about Japanese "dumping" in Canada, decided that if they couldn't beat 'em, they'd join 'em. This patriotism mixed with a solid business approach to the fast buck was expressed by Earl Smith, marketing manager for Canadian Westinghouse: "We wish the voluntary quota was one tube, so Canadian industry would be more protected. But if Japanese tubes are going to be sold in Canada it might as well be by us."

The speed with which both CGE and Canadian Westinghouse have made deals with Japanese manufacturers to import tubes into Canada shows up the seriousness of their opposition to Japanese dumping. But further, it is American tube imports into Canada that caused the greatest problems, and on this matter neither of these giants has anything to say—mainly because it is their parent firms that are doing the dumping. CGE and Westinghouse are the largest importers of American electronic tubes into Canada.

Between 1963 and 1969, while Canadian production had dropped in half to about 31 per cent of the market, the Japanese share rose from 13 to 27 per cent. However, this still leaves about 42 per cent of the market controlled by, as the brief states, "others." Since the EIA is dominated by such so-called Canadian companies as General Electric and Westinghouse, it is perhaps not so strange that they seem unconcerned about the other 42 per cent. For the most part the "others" are imports from the plants of the parent company in the United States or their European subsidiaries.

Both General Electric and Westinghouse import and export to themselves around the world. GE, for example, operates 309 subsidiaries in 30 countries and Westinghouse has 68 in 12 countries. One plant, or for that matter one country, is neither here nor there. They appear to be quite up-tight and nationalist when it comes to Japan, but generally speaking they are internationalist in their outlook. In the conclusions of their brief, the EIA appealed for government action only against the Japanese.

Moreover, since the government is only investigating the dumping of complete TV sets on the Canadian market, it will presumably not be concerned with the lucrative arrangements Westinghouse and GE have made with the Japanese exporters of tubes and component parts. No wonder the EIA is "gratified."

In the meantime, the real problems that the Canadian electronics industry faces are completely ignored. The Canadian government simply doesn't give a damn what manufacturers do or "reflect any particular concern for the electronic-component industry." No PR man has thought his way around that yet. Perhaps someone can invoke an Emergency Industrial Measures Act.

For several years the government has been bombarded with appeals and briefs by the United Electrical Workers Union, whose members must now bear the brunt of the collapse of the industry.

In 1969 the union told the government: "There appears to be a trend towards rationalization of production on the part of these multinational corporations on a world-wide scale. We think the almost total manufacture of portable, transistorized home-entertainment products in Asia is evidence of this. It is our opinion that a decision has been made to phase out tube manufacture in Canada and we have little evidence to show that other product lines are being introduced to provide continued employment for the workers involved, as was promised by the companies at meetings in the past."

The government said and did nothing.

In 1970, after General Electric announced plans to phase out manufacturing of electronic tubes at one of its Toronto plants and to discontinue completely its manufacture of colour picture tubes in Canada, the union was back to see the government and said:

"The multinational corporate parents of the Canadian companies involved have seized upon government inaction in relation to the import problem facing the industry as an excuse to chop off production in Canada summarily. This is the case even though a viable market exists for another seven to ten years. This is time in which new products could be developed that would utilize the skills or allow the re-training of those presently employed in the industry, transferring them gradually as tube manufacture tapered off."

Again the government did nothing, although a week earlier the minister in charge of astute observations on self-evident truths, J. J. Greene, did tell his friends in the oil business something which could be construed as supporting Canadian industry: "If we want to use cheap dumped goods from all over the world we won't have any kind of industry anywhere," the man said.

The union again issued an appeal: "Tube manufacture is only the tip of the iceberg. Once it goes, other sections of the industry will be chipped away. It is vital that Canada maintain an independent, comprehensive electronics industry if it is to be a technologically advanced industrial country."

This appeal was received with thunderous waves of apathy by the cabinet.

Now, down at Canadian General Electric, where progress is the most important product, layoffs are the most important by-product of progress.

And, if one still happens to be employed at Canadian Westinghouse, where one can always be sure, one can't be sure of anything any more.

Computers: Caught in the Continental Web
by Richard Liskeard

The historian Harold Innis devised what is probably the most significant theory of Canadian communications, as related to the survival of the nation.

Briefly, it runs like this: Canada, in order to survive, must link itself horizontally along the 49th parallel. Canada ceases to be a political entity when communications lines go north-south. On the basis of this, he calls the building of the CPR in the nineteenth century the *sine qua non* of the Canadian nation.

This theory became the basis of all Canadian nationalism, both conservative and socialist. Both these political groups allied to found the Canadian Broadcasting Corporation, an electronic CPR, on the theory that otherwise American broadcasting would kill us. The National Film Board and Air Canada are similar pieces of government legislation that are *per se* economically illogical, but politically critical if you start from the premise that you must keep the nation a political reality. The traditional enemy of this view, as George Grant points out in *Lament for a Nation,* is the Liberal continentalist—the politician who says economics cannot be interfered with.

In a small report issued in the summer of 1971, the Science Council, a government advisory group like the Economic Council, declared the computer data flows of this country to be on the verge of being lost to the US, and stated that an "east-west" flow of data must be established by the government at all costs, linking it in urgency to the past need to build a CPR and a CBC. The Science Council called this one of the nation's top priorities.

Compared to the great debates that preceded the CPR and the CBC, the crisis has crept up on most Canadians. The report may sound alarmist. The fault lies at least partially with the press. First of all, the papers paid scant attention to

*Published in the *Last Post,* November 1971.

the publication of the council's report. Only two smaller-town papers wrote editorials on its appearance. It has, in short, been buried. Secondly, the growing crisis facing the computer industry, and the magnitude of its implications, were never even touched on by the press.

A previous report of the Science Council noted that "the electronic computer may well be the basis in the 1970s of the world's third largest industry, after petroleum and automobiles, and just as these existing industrial complexes have wrought innumerable industrial changes in contemporary society, so the computer industry will play a major role in shaping the society of tomorrow."

The report wasn't exaggerating.

The computer industry is the world's fastest growing industry. World-wide revenue for it has grown from $975 million (US) in 1960 to $10 billion in 1969—more than a tenfold increase.

By 1974, it's expected to more than double from that to $24 billion.

A British example dramatizes it another way: by 1980 it's predicted that the computer industry will approach four per cent of the gross national product. In France it's expected to overtake that country's large automobile industry by 1976.

In Canada it's projected that by 1979, if our GNP is estimated then at $145 billion, the computer industry might be up to five per cent of that GNP. By way of comparison, we spent four per cent of our GNP on new cars in 1968.

This makes it all sound peaches for Canada's computer industry, much of it concentrated in Calgary (because of the oil industry). Growth. Profits. Markets. No fundamental factor seems to bar the road.

But instead, it's reeling. Or as the Science Council put it: "The Technology of Technologies is sick in Canada."

Canadian computer firms are beginning to die like flies. Takeovers by American data giants are happening as regular as clockwork. One estimate is that Canadian computer firms have suffered a 30 per cent decline in business. In Calgary in 1970, about three hundred people are estimated to have lost their jobs in that city's computer industry alone. In Kitchener-Waterloo, over forty highly trained computer-programmers are listed with the unemployment office. A national estimate is as yet impossible to arrive at. It has reached the proportions of an industrial crisis, in the assessment of the Science Council, an organization not usually noted for alarmist tendencies.

Calgary subsidiaries of US oil companies send their data in the form of magnetic tape or telephone lines to parent firms' computers in the US. The processed data comes back to Canada and is charged duty on the cost of the tape—$30 to $40.

This isn't restricted to the oil industry. The key point is that what has hit a hundred other industries that have high American ownership here has hit the computer industry too. An American firm, almost invariably a subsidiary, will use either the facilities of the parent firm or the subsidiary in Canada of the computer company that the oil company's parent company uses in the States. Keeps the billing simple.

The process is illustrated by what's happening to Canada's ad agencies—over a dozen have folded in a period of three years through the following mechanism: If Ford in the US has an account with an agency in New York, then Ford in Canada uses as its ad agency the Canadian subsidiary of the New York ad firm. Foreign ownership reaches its own cruising speed in the victim territory—the effects of foreign ownership extend far beyond who owns the plant itself. It affects the development of the entire industrial sector.

If Canadian ad agencies fold, so do supportive graphics industries; freelance photographers are forced out of work; copywriters are driven out of the market.

The Science Council's report recognizes this: "The creation of source material for services, such as information banks and computer-assisted learning, would migrate to the points of supply of these services. Thus much of the information and many of the ideas and values which underpin our society would eventually become largely alien. The Science Council, as a group of concerned and informed Canadians, considers these trends to be unacceptable."

Not only are supportive industries (everything from the companies that make computer cards to electronics firms that make the circuits, to fine metal firms that make the bodies, to the electricians whose skills provide the construction, to the university engineering faculties that research and provide the trained manpower) going to die off with the nub industry dying, but much more. Accessibility to data transmission and data banks plays a large role in determining where a new industry will locate. If there isn't a good terminal in Quebec City, a company won't be too interested in locating in the economically depressed Gaspé. A computer trunk line is a road. And you don't build an industry where a road doesn't extend.

But we're talking about even more dangerous implications. To understand the threat of not having national control of the computer industry and the data network, we must understand the vast implications of computers.

The US DATRAN company has predicted a volume of some 8,000 computer communications 'calls', or transactions *per second* in the United States by 1980. An article in *Fortune* has predicted that 50 per cent of US computers will be interconnected by 1974. Britain expects 50,000 computer terminals by 1973 and half a million by 1983—that's active computer data units, each an outlet of its own, like a telephone, seeking information from each other and from central data banks. By 1980, DATRAN predicts, there will be 2.5 million data terminals in the US.

The trick will be not whether you have a computer, but who has the massive data banks. Universities in the United States are already linking specialized information pools. A chemical data bank is linked to a biological data bank, for the smaller computers anywhere to query either or both.

Central data banks are assembled where there is a vast network of computers worth serving. If Canada does not assemble its data banks, it will have to plug into American data banks and we'll have to file our information into American pools. The real power in this system lies in who controls what goes in and out of the banks. As in many things, it's not the information itself that frequently determines the product, but what kind of information is gathered, and how it's assembled and joined. If every Canadian university didn't have a library of its own, it would have to depend on US university libraries, and on whether or not they felt like building up Canadian history sections. Medical students go where the best medical faculties and libraries are. A computer data bank is analogous.

It's critical not only to build up banks, but much more vital to build up a central network of access to the banks. For this reason, the Science Council report states that it is imperative to create a "National Spine," with branch lines, linking an east-to-west network, or it will flow north-south.

From his desk in downtown Ottawa, Dr. Hans Jacob von Baeyer, head of the federal task force on computer communications, pulls a full-page ad from the *Calgary Albertan*, announcing extension of the Cybernet data-centre network into Canada.

Cybernet is a US-based computer system with a linked chain of giant computers and data banks in Washington, New York, Cleveland, Chicago, Los Angeles and other big US cities. Customers in any one of these points can rent use of part or all of the facilities, and that allows them free access to the entire multimillion-dollar network.

The *Albertan* ad meant that Calgary computer users would have partial access to Cybernet's US-based equipment. Of course, even with a healthy Canadian system, there would be massive intercourse between Canadian and American data banks—Canada can't try to assemble the last word on everything and hide itself from the data banks of the world. But that's not the danger lurking in the Cybernet ad.

A Calgary subscriber to Cybernet would get services for the same price as a subscriber in Palo Alto, California—despite the added distance from the computers.

Somebody has scribbled the word "dumping" beside this paragraph in the ad in Baeyer's hands.

That term is normally applied to more tangible commodities, and refers to selling an item in a foreign country below the price in the country where it's made. In Canada, most dumping is illegal.

Should a US company be able to sell computer services cheaply in Canada because their biggest costs are already paid for by their US operations? If such unrestricted competition is allowed, Canadian firms, who have higher costs, will go under in no time. And that's exactly what's happening.

Baeyer says he isn't sure whether anti-dumping laws could be applied to selling information—which is what Cybernet does.

The Science Council's thin forty-two-page report is historic in its importance because it drops the statement that chills most of Ottawa: *"It will be necessary to restrict the free play of market forces."* Careers have been ruined for lesser slips in the cafeterias of the civil service.

The analysis contained in this document falls short in few places, but merits close attention.

Noting the healthy start the Canadian computer industry got in the fifties, it goes on to state: "This initial effort has been replaced by branch-plant manufacturing sustained by tariff barriers and industrial incentive funds. Canadian participation in the broad range of opportunities for hardware development and manufacture has been extremely small, and the software and computer-service industries are generally weak and shaky. Most of our computer-service bureaus are reporting annual losses and several have been taken over by US firms. (The lion's share of revenues... is enjoyed by foreign-owned computer firms.) ..."

The report names the following causes for this malaise:

Foreign competition
Small and scattered markets
Industrial fragmentation
The effects of Canadian geography
High costs

"The Council feels," the report states, "that branch-plant status for the Canadian computer industry is just not good enough.

"Leaving aside questions of exports, excessive dependence on foreign suppliers and lack of worthwhile jobs for highly educated Canadians, we are above all faced with the urgent need to exercise control over the shape and thrust of industry, so that its development may be harmonised with our social priorities." Mark, that last sentence refers to all industry, not just the computer industry.

Predicting that by building our own national computer-communications network "we will make a radical change in the mental resources of our society," the report adds: "...because of the pervasive influence of computers on social and cultural affairs, on national unity and on our sense of national identity we feel that Canadians *must* be able to control fully the development of computer communications networks in Canada."

The report argues for a national spinal communications network, tying together regional subnetworks, controlled by a single organization, with government participation and regulation.

It notes that "no long-range commitments to build [such a network] of a scale comparable to the commitments made in the United States. . . have been announced by Canadian organizations. Thus, in the absence of government initiatives, it seems likely that Canadian computer-communications facilities will remain essentially in their present state for some time to come."

Dr J. Kates, president of one Canadian computer firm, SETAK, Ltd., has said that there may be substantially *no* Canadian computer-service industry five years hence if the operating climate of these companies is not greatly improved.

The council warns of the results:

A continual outflow of funds for network charges to the US "of a magnitude and growth rate largely beyond our control";

Little control by Canadians of privacy and security standards (most Canadian life-insurance firms already store their private data on customers in US banks with parent companies; the possibilities of an international credit-control system are staggering; and we already know about the RCMP and how jealously it keeps its data from the FBI—it doesn't take much to extrapolate into defence and political information);

Little opportunity for Canadian bodies even to verify that advertised standards of privacy and security are in fact being met;

Cheaper service from US points, leading to the decline or death of our industry; and

Social implications of basic information being calibrated to US views, priorities and standards, thus affecting our own.

The report, in its description of the problem, is magnificent, even eloquent. It becomes disappointing in the solution it demands.

The need for a National Spine, with subtrunks to get the service to more outlying areas, is critical. But the ownership of such a vastly powerful system is even more critical. The report suggests a private organization with federal regulation—presumably similar to Bell Telephone—or the federal government holding "a controlling interest" in a mixed public-private venture.

It has been suggested that the Science Council, already fearful of having made radical suggestions, played 'conservative' on this recommendation.

What in fact the council has done is make the most eloquent case of the desperate need for nationalization of the computer industry, and for its being conducted in the national interest in a manner similar to a crown corporation such as the CBC. Allying with private enterprise is merely to give such private companies cosy participation and handouts in what is going to have to be a massive investment effort by the public purse.

CTV is a privately owned but federally regulated body, and it has devised every conceivable stratagem to put out cheap and useless Canadian television content, drowning us in one-man quiz shows with sound-track audiences as a guise for importing American programming. It has contributed relatively little to the encouragement and building of Canadian talent and resource. We will get a CTV of information systems under the Science Council's timid backing-off at the last, crucial step.

The council may be forgiven for anticipating that any Liberal or Conservative, and probably NDP government would fear to nationalize in this area where nationalization is so critically needed, because such a move would be a recognition of the need to have government control of key economic and social sectors. That would open floodgates—energy resources, dying media, etc. Might spread.

Weapons for the World: Made in Canada
by Mark Starowicz

The arms merchants

Since 1945, there have been 55 wars of significant size and duration throughout the world, and an international arms trade that has fed off them to the tune of several billion dollars. Between 1950 and 1968, according to the Institute for Strategic Studies in London (a sort of British RAND Corporation of which Lester B. Pearson is honorary president), the international trade in arms grew from $2.4 billion to $5 billion. The trade in the West alone—primarily between NATO countries—will reach an estimated $10 billion per year in the early 1970s—double the 1968 world figure.

In the international arms trade, of course, the United States is king.

The nerve centre of most of this Western arms trade is in Washington, in Room 4E-820, a pleasantly furnished Pentagon office that is the home of the International Logistics Negotiations Section of the International Security Affairs Division of the United States Department of Defense.

The man who runs this section, America's chief arms salesman, is Henry John Kuss, Jr., a long-time civil servant.

Kuss will repeat to any visitor, as he has to countless newspaper reporters, that selling arms at the rate of $2 billion per year promotes the collective security of the West, that it furthers the idea of logistical co-operation among allies and that it offsets the cost of American troops stationed abroad. Kuss has a reputation of being highly receptive to reporters, and has no qualms about talking of his job—drumming up business for American arms manufacturers and selling surplus US munitions to foreign governments.

It's much harder to get beyond the glass door on the seventh floor of Tower B on Kent Street in Ottawa. This is the

*Published in the *Last Post*, February 1970.

International Programs Branch of the Canadian Commercial Corporation of the Department of Industry, Trade and Commerce, where Mr. D. H. Gilchrist sits in an equally pleasantly furnished office. He is director of marketing for the IP section, and Canada's chief arms salesman.

Though Mr. Gilchrist will not agree to accept visitors from the press, he can be persuaded if those who wish to see him telephone the office of the Minister of Industry, Trade and Commerce and make pointed inquiries about what it is that the International Programs Branch has to hide anyway. Then Mr. Gilchrist will see you, and provide a brief speech not unlike Mr. Kuss's about promoting collective security among allies, priming Canadian industry and offsetting imbalanced foreign trade.

After asking that he not be quoted, he will explain that the role of his office is "to make sure that Canadian salesmen get to see the right people in the defence departments" of other countries and thus "can compete for contracts."

The Canadian Commercial Corporation's role is to act as a middleman between the foreign buyer and the Canadian supplier. The foreign buyer frequently enters into a primary contract with the CCC, which then enters into a secondary contract with the Canadian company. The CCC's duties, through the various trade attaches in Canadian embassies and through special representatives, include making foreign buyers aware that the products they seek are available in Canada.

Mr. Gilchrist's International Programs Branch does precisely this work, but only in the area of arms.

The existence of the IP Branch in the Department of Industry, Trade and Commerce is unknown to most people in Ottawa, including the press gallery, and even to the minister's assistant—until he was telephoned to persuade Mr. Gilchrist to give an interview. IP was once in the Department of Defence Production, but was part of the merger of that department with Trade and Commerce. Mr. Gilchrist's desire for anonymity extended to saying flatly, "that has nothing to do with us" when asked first over the phone about the subject of arms sales.

Mr. Gilchrist, assisted by an equally nervous colleague, Mr. Janigan, insisted that his office's work is "like any other trade office's" and that they are not "merchants of death" but "defence-product specialists."

"We just try to find outside markets—that is we help Canadian companies find outside markets for that sector of industry which specializes in defence products and related equipment," he said.

"Let's face facts—as long as we have defence forces, we have to have a defence industry, and as long as we have that industry, they have to have foreign markets too.

"I mean, these companies provide for the specialized needs of the Canadian military. Other countries need the things we have developed, and so they are marketed abroad.

"But it's also obvious that the needs of the Canadian defence forces wouldn't alone support such an industry—the needs are too small or specific, and so foreign markets have to be developed to keep these specialties going."

That is why, he explained, the Defence Sharing Agreement with the United States is so useful. They get our specialized products and so do our NATO allies, and we get the products we need and are able to support industry in Canada—as able a description of an international military-industrial complex and its mechanics as anyone could offer.

Canada's specialties are in transport and communications, he pointed out, and this determines its defence production—aircraft, ground transport, radio communications, radar, computer systems and navigational aids. In these fields Canada is a recognized leader—and a major supplier to the armed forces of other countries.

If you want to buy a jet fighter or a missile-guidance system, you'll come to Canada and look up Mr. Gilchrist and he'll put you in touch with the right people. He will introduce visiting generals or arms buyers to the people at Canadair or Litton Systems. Or one of his representatives in Paris, Rome, London, Bonn or Brussels will visit your office with a set of prospectus papers, and perhaps urge Litton Systems to send an agent to you.

A testament to how well Mr. Gilchrist and his associates do their job (he'll mention this proudly as "one of our best successes") was the sale of 105 CF-5 jet fighters to the Netherlands in 1967 for $145,000,000. The Canadair and Orenda-built jet, manufactured in Canada under licence from an American firm, Northrop (where it's the F-5 "Freedomfighter") is refined much beyond the American product, and "we even outbid the original licencing company in the US for the contract."

It's possible to learn most of the amounts of sales to foreign countries, even which country spent how much—but rarely can one discover just what was bought—most of that is classified for the benefit of the contractor or the purchasing country's "security requirements."

But it's possible to get an idea.

It pays to advertise

Mr. Gilchrist will give you a pile of documents when he is finally rid of you—"this will tell you everything you want to know"—except that they are all superficial NATO propaganda and Defence Department annual reports and tell you nothing. One document he will not give you, and if you ask him for it he will say they are out of stock.

They might well be, because this document, actually a 500-page book, gets around. That's the idea.

It's called *Canadian Defence Products*, and it's a catalogue of the arms and equipment Canada has up for sale. It's neatly divided into a subject index, a list of corporations and what products they offer, and a main section which has photos and pep-talk write-ups about what wonders this jet and that machine gun can perform. All it lacks is a mail-order form.

In its introduction it states that this book has been prepared for "friendly and allied countries" and that it " ... is a collection of data covering both products and firms, arranged so as to simplify the location of sources of supply for equipment, parts or services which may be required."

The white pages just list the products and the companies who sell or service them: Guns through 30mm; Guns 75mm through 125mm, through 300mm; Chemical Weapons; Launchers, Torpedoes and Depth Charges; Nuclear Ordnance Handling and Test Equipment; Guided-Missile Warhead Components; Rockets and Ammunition; Combat Ships. They range through to radios and industrial furnaces and snowmobiles.

An interesting index heading is Group 14:

Guided Missiles

Bristol Aerospace Ltd.
Canadair Ltd.
Computing Devices of Canada Ltd.
De Havilland Aircraft (SPAR)

That means if you want a full guided missile, call any of the above. But if you just want "Gyro Components" to one, call Abex Industries, Aviation Electric, Ranar Industries or Litton Systems (Canada) Ltd. If you only want a "Guidance System" go to Computing Devices of Canada Ltd. If you want "Guided-Missile Launchers" choose Bata Engineering, Canadian Vickers, or any of five others.

If you want an air force, or if you want to equip your infantry with everything from troop transports to FN rifles, or you want an aerial-reconnaissance camera, look through the picture pages.

If you want a list of every Canadian company that is linked into defence production, leaf through the blue pages which name over 880 of them, with address and chief products.

You may recognize Dow Chemicals, CIL, Canadair, A. V. Roe, Hawker-Siddeley and the like, who have already received some publicity. But you will find some unexpected examples of free enterprise such as:

METAL FABRICATORS LTD.
102 Tillson Avenue
Tillsonburg, Ontario
President: J. D. Judge
Contact: W. A. Pollard, General Manager
Telephone:-519: 842-3621
Manufacturers of: Hospital and School Furniture and Equipment; Steel Sub-Assemblies for various products; Industrial Laboratory Equipment; Ammunition Boxes; Bomb, Depth Charge; Rocket and Guided Missile Components.

Metalite Co. Ltd. in Cap de la Madeleine, Quebec, makes toboggans, lawn furniture and small-arms ammunition components. Fairbanks-Morse in Kingston will sell you a locomotive or a torpedo launcher. Hand Chemical Industries in Milton, Ontario, will sell you flame throwers—or firecrackers.

Technology and empire

The Canadian public started becoming aware of the Defence Production Sharing Agreement between Canada and the United States five years ago, in the midst of the debate over Canadian complicity in the Vietnam war. At that time, Canadian industry produced $370,000,000 in arms and arms products for export to the United States, under Pentagon contract. Today, that trade has flourished to well beyond the $400,000,000 mark. With over $50,000,000 (1968 figure) added for foreign export other than to the United States, the price tag on the Canadian arms trade nears half a billion.

Lopping off the Defence Sharing Agreement from statistical grouping with the other foreign sales permits government officials to tell critics that its foreign arms trade is "a drop in the bucket" compared to other countries. But the division is artificial. We also have a production-sharing agreement with West Germany, yet Canada lists those sales as an arms export. We sell in the range of half a billion dollars of arms abroad—compared to two billion by the largest arms exporter in the world, the United States. Whatever we might like to consider ourselves, Canada is one of the world's major arms exporters.

Just as our defence products ended up in Vietnam after they were sold to the United States, they end up in almost every other country the United States sells arms to today.

Any salesman who depends on 80 per cent of his sales to one customer and has to tailor his entire production to the needs of that customer is, the point has often been made, under the control of that customer. But the control that the United States exercises over the Canadian arms trade is even more direct than the obvious economic mechanics of the arms picture.

In his book on the international arms trade, *The War Business* (New York, 1969), Washington journalist George Thayer demonstrates how even the Canadian arms salesmen are effectively only agents for Henry Kuss's International Logistics Negotiations office.

The Canadian defence industry is, for the most part, American owned or run. The major aircraft-manufacturing plant, Canadair in Montreal, is owned by General Dynamics Corp. Litton Systems, the computer and systems-guidance manufacturer, is simply one of the satellites in economic orbit around the Litton Industries conglomerate. But even beyond that, the aircraft we manufacture are built in Canada under licence from the original American manufacturer, as in the case of the CF-5, which is a modified version of the F-5 Freedomfighter and is manufactured in Canada under licence from the Northrop Corp.

Canadian manufacturers—and, as a result, the Canadian government—are not able to enter into a contract agreement with a foreign buyer unless it is cleared through Kuss's ILN office. Gilchrist may boast that the Dutch preferred to buy our CF-5 over Northrop's F-5, but approval of that sale still had to be given by Kuss.

There are several reasons why such an arrangement is of great advantage to the United States Defense Department, whether the purchase is made from Canada or from the US.

Former Defense Secretary Robert McNamara's program of "co-operative logistics" allowed the US to exercise greater control over what arms NATO countries produced, led to standardization of weaponry, allowed American industry to specialize, made the other NATO countries specialize to the extent that they grew interdependent on each other's parts and components and specialized technology. Furthermore, Thayer writes: "The United States benefitted because private manufacturers of armaments received income from licensing fees; it stimulated a heavy trans-Atlantic traffic in technicians and technical data that was eventually to bring more foreign-held dollars into the US Treasury."

"By 1959," he continues, "the concept of co-production was fully accepted by most industrialized Western countries as a lucrative way to re-enter the arms market." It was in 1959 that the Defence Production Sharing Agreement was signed with Canada, and we climbed on a bandwagon that has proved very profitable since.

But as 'competitors', we're far from independent. A series of events in 1965 and 1966, involving ninety Canadian-built F-86 Sabrejets, illustrates the benefit to the US of having a second-country source of American arms, and also the ineffectiveness of resale-control procedures.

The incident began in 1957 when West Germany bought 225 F-86 jets from Canada. By 1965 the Luftwaffe had moved up to the F-104 G Starfighter, and was anxious to unload the phased-out planes. In the autumn of that year, the Indians and the Pakistanis went to war over Kashmir, and a general world-wide arms embargo was clamped on both belligerents.

Shortly after the September 22 cease-fire, an arms-buying delegation from Iran arrived in Bonn, headed by General Hassan Toufanian. He was accompanied by an arms expert from the Pakistani Army, Colonel Hussein Zaidi, and this apparently raised no suspicions in Bonn.

Toufanian wanted to buy ninety of the jets and the Germans agreed to sell if conditions were met. The US resale-control procedures in a case like this require that Bonn (the current seller) obtain permission from Ottawa (the manufacturer and original seller), which in turn obtains permission from the United States (the licenser and controlling government). Assurances having been given that the jets were only for the Iranian Air Force, the deal was approved all round.

Between March and November of 1966, the jets were transferred to Iran. But they soon began appearing in Pakistan, ostensibly to be "repaired," and the Indian press complained loudly of a violation of the embargo.

Thayer notes that it was common knowledge among weapons dealers that the Canadian jets were from the start destined for Pakistan, and Senator Stuart Symington is quoted as saying during hearings on the matter: "Our own intelligence knew exactly at the time that these F-86s were meant for Pakistan."

Without Canada and West Germany as a second source of aircraft, this deal would never have been able to originate from US aircraft stock. Whether Canada was an ignorant link in the chain or fully informed is irrelevant. Arms, once produced, are seldom discarded, but enter a chain of sales and resales that ultimately means the producer is adding his product to the round-robin of the international arms market.

Footing the bill

Objections to arms sales are generally morally based, but the implications for Canada of embarking on such a giant program go beyond the dangers to our souls.

On March 12 of 1969, Ed Broadbent, the New Democrat

MP from Oshawa, gave a brief speech in the House of Commons that the government benches did not bother replying to, and which the press gallery saw fit not to report. This becomes particularly disturbing when it's considered that Broadbent was raising an issue never before discussed in the House, and an issue about which Canadians have been kept in the dark.

Broadbent charged that the government is "promoting a military-industrial elite in this country" through its research and development programs. Analyzing three government programs for aid to industrial research, he demonstrated that "the Canadian government now provides more money for research and development in the military area than it does for civilian work."

Under these three programs—the Industrial Research and Development Incentives Act (IRDIA), the Program for the Advance of Industrial Technology (PAIT) and the Defence Development Sharing Program (DDSP, created under the Defence Production Sharing pact with the US)—the government provides approximately 50 per cent of the capital costs of military research and development. But in the civilian sector all financial assistance, plus interest on the money advanced, must be repaid if projects prove commercially viable.

N. H. Lithwick, in a study of federal deployment of funds in the *Journal of Canadian Studies*, notes that over 50 per cent of federal funds going into research and development are used for military purposes. "If profits from war industries are greater than those derived from production for peace, are industrialists likely to choose the latter?" Broadbent asked. No. And that's the idea.

In the fiscal year 1964-65, $474,000 was provided under the Industry Modernization for Defence Exports programs to cover nineteen projects. By the fiscal year 1967-68, this had increased to $10.6 million covering 95 projects. An expansion in spending can also be found in the grants from the Defence Industrial Research Program of the Defence Research Board between the fiscal years 1962-63 and 1967-68.

"Most alarming of all," Broadbent said in his speech, "are the figures relating to the Defence Development Sharing Program." He cites that in the fiscal year 1961-62, the government spent $4.4 million on thirty-three military development projects. "By 1968 this had increased to $23 million and 53 projects," said Broadbent. These are direct government grants to private industry for work on military projects, mostly for the US.

But Mr. Broadbent's figures are not the whole story. They are the government's published figures, and they succeed in making omissions by judicious shifting of classifications to other categories.

Made available to us through a member of the minister's office at the Department of Industry, Trade and Commerce is a document entitled *Canada-US Defence-Production Sharing, Development Co-operation Contracts* and marked "Confidential."

The fourteen-page document is a list of all military co-operation projects Canada and the US have shared costs on between 1959 and 1967. It breaks the classifications down by project, contractor in Canada, which US service or corporation sponsors the project, funds contributed by the Canadian contractor involved, US funds, other allied funds and Canadian government funds.

It lists the following grants per year:

Year	Projects	US Funds (tot.)	Canadian Gov't Funds (tot.)
1959	11	$4,330,809	nil
1960	30	1,035,791	$ 5,449,685
1961	51	6,263,281	11,788,117
1962	34	8,919,078	10,462,673
1963	29	1,905,218	12,550,215
1964	34	8,043,516	27,785,229
1965	46	5,018,407	19,553,348
1966	36	8,688,113	26,919,014
1967	36	7,395,303	30,559,866

This means that Canada spent a total of $145,068,148 between the time the agreement went into effect and 1967 to subsidize the production of arms in Canada for the United States and abroad.

It is clear that the Department of Industry has decided to promote defence industries on the grounds that it is politically expedient. In its program review for 1969-70, the department concluded that independent Canadian production of all our defence needs would be uneconomic. It rejected the conclusion that we should purchase defence equipment abroad, and argued that to buy on the basis of the lowest rates in world markets would "deprive Canadian industry of a vital source of advancement, not to mention annual exports currently of the order of half a billion dollars."

Mr. Gilchrist will argue further that it allows Canada to develop resources of technical expertise, and that the expertise spills out to civilian production and nurtures the entire industrial sector.

It does. Canada also becomes more dependent on the technical expertise of other NATO countries, particularly the US, and the development of Canadian industry is directed by the fact that our prime technological research is military based and grows in that mold, becoming more and more dependent on the defence-production sector.

In short, the technology becomes international and interlocking—McNamara's aim in his co-production scheme. The pivot and the driving force for industrial expansion becomes the military needs of the United States and the Western military establishment. Where the technology goes, the economy is soon to follow, with the politics not far behind.

The NHL Power Play
by Nick Auf der Maur

"The NHL never has been motivated by what its customers might or might not like. It has been guided by its estimate of what the public will hold still for."
— Jim Proudfoot, Toronto Daily Star.

"This is a ripe issue, a nationalist issue. The same issue we're going to face with Arctic oil, the Mackenzie pipeline, water, you name it. It's a question of a natural resource getting sold out. Hell, three of the companies that make hockey sticks are now owned by Americans. Unless the business community and everybody else start supporting this thing, the game will go right out the window."
— Chris Lang of Hockey Canada, Feb. 1971

When it comes to hockey, there's a general if inarticulate malaise amongst Canadians. There's a feeling that something has happened to their national game, what Ralph Allen once called their national religion.

It's something that creeps into tavern conversations, magazines and radio and TV shows, but almost never on to the sports pages, at least not in the two senior NHL cities.

The malaise began to manifest itself with expansion, but its roots go beyond that.

The National Hockey League was organized in 1917 by five teams—Ottawa, Toronto, Quebec City and two from Montreal.

In 1971, the NHL comprised fourteen teams—three in Canada and eleven in the United States. In between, the league attained complete monopoly control of almost all organized hockey in Canada. The NHL ship is so tightly organized that even the robber barons of old couldn't have devised a more monopolistic, feudal set-up.

In the early and middle sixties, the big powers in the NHL were Conn Smythe of the Toronto Maple Leafs; Frank

*Published in the *Last Post*, May 1971.

Selke, general manager of the Montreal Canadiens, owned by Senator Hartland Molson: and James Norris, owner of the Chicago Black Hawks. Norris had also owned the Detroit Red Wings and part of the New York Rangers, as well as the Montreal Forum. But US anti-trust laws forced him to get rid of the Red Wings (he sold the franchise to his half-brother) and the Rangers, while also breaking up his International Boxing Club with which he had monopolized that sport.

With these men in power, Clarence Campbell was a vocal opponent of expansion.

But times were changing. The old feudal lords of hockey were being eased out.

Conn Smythe eased himself out in favour of his son Stafford Smythe while Franke Selke and Senator Molson were in the process of turning the Forum and the Canadiens over to David Molson, the blond-haired, blue-eyed son.

At the same time, south of the border, a new man was on the rise. He was William Jennings, the lawyer for Graham-Paige Corp. which took over Madison Square Gardens from Norris's boxing empire. He soon became president of the Rangers.

Jennings, an American with no previous experience in hockey, started pushing expansion. The old guard regarded the NHL as a private club, one that made a lot of money. They were content. But the young Turks, led by Jennings, saw the possibility of turning the NHL into a really big, American money-making enterprise.

Before long, Clarence Campbell, the old traditionalist, was espousing visions of a greatly expanded league, putting hockey up on a par with US pro football, baseball and basketball. In 1967, in one fell swoop, the NHL doubled its size, adding six new franchises at $2,000,000 a throw.

James Norris and the old Canadian traditionalists were reluctant. They favoured adding two new teams at first, to preserve the quality of the game. Toronto and Montreal agreed, so long as they didn't have to split their Canadian TV money with any new Canadian team. (Actually Stafford Smythe told the city of Vancouver that if they would turn over a downtown block for $1 he would provide an arena and a franchise. The city thought the price steep and was frozen out.)

James Norris was persuaded to go along when the cup was sweetened. He owned the arena in St. Louis, a city that hadn't applied for an NHL franchise. Although several groups in Vancouver would have gladly paid the $2,000,000 admission, the BC city wasn't awarded a franchise. St. Louis got one and the league went about trying to find someone to pay the $2,000,000 and buy Norris's arena. They hit it lucky when Sid Salomon III persuaded his father to ante up. Ironically, St. Louis has become the most successful expansion team.

While the original six team owners pocketed millions, the new teams each were allowed to draft twenty of the least-wanted players in the NHL. Of the original 120 players drafted in 1967, only twenty-four are still playing with the same teams.

As a result of expansion, the quality of play in the league was diluted. Further expansion in 1970 saw the addition of Vancouver and Buffalo, this time at the price of $6,000,000 each—triple the old cost.

The price was so steep that no local Vancouver businessmen could raise the dough. So in stepped the Medical Investment Corporation of Minneapolis, a company originally set up as tax shelter for five Minnesota doctors. Among other things, it owns the Ice Follies and several radio and TV stations.

Medicor, as it's known, bought the Vancouver Canucks and set up shop in a new arena, one built and paid for by federal, provincial and municipal money.

While this was going on, William Jennings was wheeling and dealing in New York, setting himself up as the new power in the NHL. With Americans owning eleven of the fourteen teams in the NHL, he found no difficulty. (Norris had died in the interim, leaving William Wirtz to take over.)

The NHL set up a new office in New York, run by Don Ruck, a former Connecticut newspaperman. Ruck also set up NHL Services, a money-producing outfit dealing in endorsements, games, souvenirs and similar products. Control was slipping away from Canada.

The league headquarters was kept in Montreal for two reasons. First, because the labour pool—the players—comes from Canada and it's easier to control out of a Canadian city. But most important, Canada provides what Clarence

Campbell calls a "hospitable climate."

He patriotically explained that Canada provides protection from "harassment in the US by various types of Congressional or legislative investigations and so on." The "so on" refers to US anti-trust laws which forbid monopolies.

Meanwhile, according to Jennings, the next cities in line for NHL teams were Cleveland, Atlanta, Kansas City and—believe it or not—Hempstead, Long Island.

To a lot of people, rapid expansion has killed the game. For the most part, it's played before fans who know little or nothing about hockey except the fighting. Stick-handling, passing, finesse and grace have all but been eliminated says Maurice Richard. Hockey used to be a game of puck control. Now the teams dump it into the corners and scramble. A recent survey showed that close to 70 per cent of goals scored in the NHL come from "second efforts."

That means from rebounds and, mostly, scrambles inside the blueline. There is less and less of the well-executed, coordinated play as one team carries the puck in. Old-time Canadian fans are losing interest. In their stead, the new fans—the less discerning ones with a greater consumer potential—are being recruited in Minneapolis and Los Angeles. But none of this means that the Molsons and the Bassetts are losing any money—they're laughing.

In 1969, the stock of the Canadian Arena Company (which owns the Canadiens), which had been selling in the neighbourhood of $775 per share, was split fifty to one.

"David Molson," said lawyer H. W. Hamilton at the time, "has always felt that the company belongs to the people, but with stock at $900, there's little chance of them owning any of it."

The company made a net profit of $939,000 in 1969. Three Molson sons own 57 per cent of the stock.

Over in Toronto, Maple Leaf Gardens reported net profits, after taxes, of $987,795.

In 1969, president Stafford Smythe and vice-president Harold Ballard were hauled before the courts on charges of income-tax evasion.

Smythe was alleged to have evaded income taxes on $278,920—including $208,166 appropriated by him from Maple Leaf Gardens Ltd. for construction and improvements on his residence and $35,575 for personal and family expenses.

In 1970 the new Leaf president, G. E. Mara, and David Molson of the Canadiens showed up at a Senate committee hearing to denounce tax reforms.

At present, corporations buy "a substantial number" of season tickets en bloc (all but 1000 of the Forum's 16,500 seats are held by season subscribers, while in Toronto there's a waiting list of 3000 people, some of whom have been waiting for six or seven years for season tickets). So the ordinary fan doesn't have much of a chance of seeing a game in a good seat, unless he has friends, corporate friends.

The white paper on taxation would prohibit corporations from deducting the cost of such tickets from their income tax. Incredibly, Molson and Mara claimed such a move would drive them into bankruptcy.

"Hockey is not only Canada's national sport," said the patriotic Mr. Mara, "it is a way of life of countless citizens, young and old, and beyond doubt, contributes in a multitude of ways to the building of young men, to the social structure and to the basic fibre of our people."

Besides, said the two magnates of Canadian hockey, if that particular clause wasn't eliminated from the tax reforms, they'd sell out to the Americans.

The prohibition of tax-deductible tickets, said Molson, "would probably lead to the deterioration in the operations of the Forum generally and inevitably acquisition by United States interests of the Montreal franchise."

But most of all, they were there to speak out against the tax proposals, said Mara, because they did not want to see Canada "degenerate into just another colourless, static socialist state."

So much for the basic fibre of our people.

The basic ingredient behind the money-making success of the NHL magnates is the fact that they have just about everybody in Canada, or at least all the kids on skates, working for them.

All of hockey is set up pyramid fashion. While the intent of amateur hockey may be sports and fun, its real function is to train players for ultimate service in the NHL while weeding out those with lesser talent.

From the ages of about six to twelve, just about any kid

can play in some sort of organized hockey. Afterwards, it becomes progressively tougher because everything is set up to eliminate kids who are just in it for simple sport.

This is why in one community there may be, say, nine pee-wee teams. The next year the players advance to bantam—but there's only one bantam team for the players from last year's nine pee-wee teams. Some make it, and the rest are out of luck if they want to continue playing hockey.

In Montreal, the NHL has a central registry, a computer data-bank system, containing the names and particulars of every hockey player over the age of twelve in Canada. This is not done for the service of amateur sport, naturally, but to facilitate an orderly draft system—some call it a cattle auction.

NHL control over amateur hockey goes a long way back and was well documented by the government task force on hockey which culminated in the setting up of Hockey Canada. But that's another story.

A good illustration of how this all came about is contained in the Jean Béliveau story, the one the sports pages forgot to mention when they eulogized "le Gros Bill" on his farewell night in Montreal.

Back in the early fifties, Jean Béliveau was the biggest thing in Quebec City since another game was lost on the Plains of Abraham.

Béliveau was playing for the Quebec Citadelles, a junior team. As an amateur in 1950-51, he grossed $20,000—half from the team and, reportedly, half from a milk company.

At age nineteen, he was the idol of Quebec City. Le Colisée, a new arena the size of many NHL rinks, was built to handle the crowds he attracted. The following year he was moved up to the Quebec Aces of the Senior League, also an amateur league, but the Canadiens, under Frank Selke, were out to get Béliveau.

A minor war festered between the professionals in Montreal and the businessmen who ran amateur hockey in Quebec. Béliveau was king of Quebec and there was little incentive the Canadiens could offer to lure him away. In 1951-52 he signed with the Aces. So long as he remained amateur, the Canadiens couldn't get him. The next year it was the same thing, thanks to the Aces' wily coach, Punch Imlach.

But Frank Selke was determined.

During the next season, the Canadiens exerted pressure in the proper places to persuade the other teams in the Senior League to turn professional. In the summer of 1953, the representatives of the Quebec Senior League, with the exception of Punch Imlach, voted to turn professional. Finally the Canadiens were able to annex Béliveau, signing him to an unheard-of—at that time—contract for five years.

Until roughly that time, senior hockey was big in all of Canada. Towns like Sudbury were able to enjoy good, live hockey. And the fans flocked in to make it a financial success.

But by the early fifties, the NHL was moving into a monopoly position and senior leagues started to die.

In those days, any kid playing organized hockey from the age of twelve had to sign a card making him the property of a professional team in whose territory he played. It was all part of a deal signed with the Canadian Amateur Hockey Association in 1940.

In return, the NHL teams operated elaborate farm systems to develop their players. Years later this system was replaced with the modern draft, instituted in full in 1967.

The main purpose in setting up the draft was to equalize the calibre of the twelve-team NHL, but it also served the best interests of the old teams, which were getting bogged down in the messy sponsorship system. Under the new arrangement, the NHL pays the CAHA a set price for every player drafted by the pros.

But the pyramid set-up and the NHL control of the game from top to bottom still hold true. Everything works with the view of supplying the NHL with an abundant and developed supply of labour.

In Quebec, for instance, there are more than 50,000 boys sixteen years and under playing organized hockey. Beyond that age the number shrinks dramatically, not because there isn't a desire to continue playing but because it becomes inefficient for the development of NHL material.

The CAHA is so structured that it can provide organization and facilities only for those with promise.

As a result, hockey is permeated with the NHL philosophy. In Toronto recently, the father of a seven-year-old boy showed the press a letter he received from the Don Valley amateur hockey organization.

The letter promised equipment to the boy if he made their team, tickets to all Marlboro Junior A games, admission to a Leafs' practice and the promise of a trip which would be "the highlight of the boy's minor-hockey-league career."

If a kid is good enough, at the age of fifteen or sixteen he gets to play junior hockey, which usually spells the end of his education. The Ontario Junior A league claims 90 per cent of its players manage to keep up their studies, while in Quebec the figure is much lower. However, recent studies have shown that the average player manages to keep up school averages while playing hockey full time only until the eleventh grade. After that, he usually becomes a scholastic disaster.

By the time he's twenty, with no marketable skills except the ability to wield a hockey stick, the big boob is ready for the pros. A lot of them don't make it after they get that far, and they're chucked out and left to their own devices.

But if he's lucky, he'll get drafted and either make the grade in the NHL directly or, as is usual, get to play in Omaha or Tulsa or any of the other forty-five or so minor professional teams operating in North America.

After that it's the big time. Oakland or Pittsburgh. Or something.

Part Three
The Politics of Last Resort

What hope there was for some kind of action from the Trudeau government on foreign ownership was pinned on Herb Gray. For almost three years, the government was able to say the question was "under study" by this bright young economic wizard with the wooden face.

Gray's labour, of course, produced something only slightly larger than a tiny mouse, and even then the government refused to publish it. The Gray report was finally leaked in early 1972 by *Canadian Forum*.

But if the Gray report amounted to little, the government's final proposals made in summer 1972 for a 'policy' on foreign investment amounted to even less. Many shared economist Mel Watkins's scoff: "It's a joke!" The reaction from the domestic and foreign business interests was so unruffled as to prove an embarrassment to the government.

But all this was hardly surprising to anyone who had followed the career of Herb Gray, particularly just before he was hoisted to cabinet level. In December of 1969, in its inaugural issue, the *Last Post* carried an article on Herb Gray and the Ford Motor Company. That article is the first chapter in this section, and it makes interesting reading with the aid of hindsight.

The debate over foreign investment and the Gray report was a minor problem to the Trudeau government compared with the events of August 1971.

On August 15, Richard Nixon took America's trading partners by surprise by imposing a series of stiff economic measures to control inflation. He imposed a ten per cent surtax on most imports, concentrating chiefly on manufactured goods. And he told America's trading partners in almost as many words that they were exploiting the United States. Chief on the list of exploiters were Japan and Canada.

The surtax was a temporary measure to force the realignment of world currencies. Faced with other countries' refusal to revalue their currencies upwards, and reluctant to devalue the American dollar, Nixon in effect forced a ten per cent devaluation of other countries' currencies as far as imports were concerned. With this club in hand, Treasury Secretary Connolly went off to meet the Big Ten and demanded concessions in exchange for lifting the surtax.

The ways in which Canada was wronging the United States were revealed when Washington leaked a 'shopping list' of grievances through the *Chicago Tribune*. Chief on the list was the auto pact. Washington claimed that Canada was profiting unduly from the special exemptions in the pact, and was shipping too many cars and parts into the US.

Another key item on the list was the question of arms: Washington complained that Ottawa was buying nowhere near the amount of arms that the US was buying from Canada. An Ottawa trade official is said to have remarked wryly to his American counterpart: "Sorry about the arms thing; should we start our own Viet Nam war to rectify the trade balance?"

A third demand was that Canada drop its restrictions against its citizens bringing more than a certain amount of goods back from the US duty free.

Ottawa fumbled, obviously hard up for any response to make. The Trudeau government took a conciliatory line, suggesting, for example, that the exemptions in the auto pact were only "symbolic" and therefore expendable.

But the Nixon squeeze was not over. Washington launched a domestic incentives program, DISC, which encouraged domestic production and penalized production in branch plants of American corporations abroad. As a direct result of this program, Ford and Chrysler ultimately moved the manufacture of certain auto parts back south across the border. The wage freeze imposed in the US began leaking across the border as branch plants of American corporations refused to bargain with unions in Canada beyond the guidelines set for the American market. And the war of words grew daily as Treasury Secretary Connolly dropped all diplomatic language in his war with America's trading partners.

It all added up to a nightmare for the Trudeau government, powerless to control its export policy, powerless to control the impact on Canadian jobs, powerless in the face of Canadian manufacturers demanding action, powerless in the face of the nationalists who were saying we-told-you-so.

As the second chapter in this section shows, the government resorted to brave talk—Canadians were given to believe that Ottawa was defying Washington. While America's other trading partners were being blackmailed into revaluing their currencies upwards, Ottawa made much ado about its having floated the dollar without revaluation. A few months later, this illusion was dissipated when the Canadian dollar rose to three cents above the American dollar; meanwhile, talk about removing the safeguards from the auto pact disappeared, clearly because Ottawa had capitulated on the currency front.

Here was a time of reckoning for Canada. And, as the review in chapter two of decades of Liberal economic policy indicates, it was a time long in coming.

One of the corollaries of this economic policy is regional disparity. As previous chapters have shown, it's difficult to set national economic goals in a foreign-dominated economy. It may be one of our national goals to develop the under-industrialized Maritime region, but how are you going to persuade a company to establish there?

The answer the Trudeau government came up with was "The Great Canadian DREE Machine." the subject of the third chapter in this section. The Department of Regional Economic Expansion under Jean Marchand pumped millions into already wealthy corporations, many of them foreign owned, to 'persuade' them to locate in depressed regions.

DREE emerges with a sad, and often very curious record.

And where does this leave us?

It leaves us fourteen years further advanced on the road of "economic domination" as outlined in 1958 in an article in *Cité Libre*.

The article, which attacks the Liberals and Conservatives for allowing Canada to become "...a colony exploited without limit," was written by Pierre Elliott Trudeau, and comprises the last chapter of this book.

Ford Has a Better Idea
by John Zaritsky

In the fall of 1969, after Herb Gray was appointed to the cabinet as a minister without portfolio, nobody laughed when the Windsor East MP's special duties were described as keeping watch on US investment in Canada.

Everybody had forgotten how Herb had been cheering for his good friends, the Ford Motor Company of Canada Ltd., when the Commons Public Accounts Committee investigated why the US-controlled firm had been 'forgiven' more than $75 million in duties it owed Ottawa.

But that had happened way back in the spring when the Trudeau government, still making loud noises about tightening the belt to fight inflation, didn't want anybody to find out how they threw away $75 million in taxes.

There were, in fact, a lot of things that the Liberals and Gray would have liked the Canadian public to stop wondering about in its dealings with Ford.

There was the matter of a curious lapse of time between the point at which the auditor-general blew the whistle on Ford and reported how much they owed in duties for failure to meet the requirements of the 1965 Canada-US auto pact—and the point eighteen months later when the Trudeau cabinet quietly got around to forgiving Ford the debt.

Nobody really knows why it took the Liberal government so long to take action, but some observers note that sandwiched halfway between the start and the close of the Ford affair came the June 1968 election.

To obtain a glimmer of how well Herb Gray could be expected to behave as a Canadian economic nationalist, a review of the Ford hearings—and some facts the daily press chose, for their own reasons, to ignore—raises interesting points.

The 1965 auto pact, which provided for limited free trade in cars and parts between Canada and the United States, laid

*Published in the *Last Post*, December 1969.

down certain conditions Canadian auto makers had to meet in order to avoid customs duties.

On the day the pact was signed, Ford's president, Karl Scott, wrote a letter to Ottawa stating that the company would have certain difficulties meeting the conditions. Few saw it strange that one of the wealthiest corporations in the country should encounter such difficulties. At any rate, Scott's letter was tabled in the House and therefore made public.

But the government's response, from then Industry Minister C. M. Drury, was not made public until it was introduced before the Public Accounts committee in June 1969.

It came out in the committee's hearings (much to Gray's obvious discomfort) that Drury replied to Scott on March 1, 1965, in the following manner: "I am confident that the government will give sympathetic consideration to Ford's problems and to your request that Ford should not be disqualified from the benefits of the automotive program."

Drury's confidence proved not to be misplaced, and on January 28, 1969, the Trudeau cabinet decided to remit $80 million owed by Ford and thirteen other companies. By an order-in-council the amounts owed and the names of the companies involved were not mentioned.

An order-in-council—a cabinet decision—does not have to be approved by Parliament, and it wasn't until weeks later that the news of the order was published (as is required) in the *Canada Gazette*, the government's official paper.

This was also curious, because it is commonly known that the *Gazette* rarely contains anything significant except letters of incorporation and the like, and therefore has virtually no public readership. The government might as well have announced it in a graveyard at midnight.

One newspaper reporter did notice, however, and that partially sparked the embarrassing committee enquiry Mr. Gray had to attend in June.

At the hearings, government officials maintained that the names of the companies and the amounts owed should be kept confidential. Committee Chairman Alfred Hales (PC—Wellington) pointed out, however, that four years earlier the government had publicly disclosed the name of another delinquent auto maker and the amount he owed.

Gray and other Liberals stated that the committee should

seek a legal opinion and consequently the release of such information (as requested by sixteen-year veteran committee member Harold Winch, NDP—Vancouver E) should be delayed. But Hales cast the deciding vote in favour of Winch's motion, and G. R. Long, assistant auditor-general, was ordered to supply the breakdown.

Winch told reporters at the time: "I was really surprised that it was so tough to get the names. Just why it was so tough is a mighty interesting question."

It proved to be. After it was revealed by Long that Ford had been forgiven $75,051,877, Liberal committee members—Mr. Gray in the lead—were sent scurrying. In Winch's words, "the government propaganda machine went into high gear."

Trade, Commerce and Industry Minister Jean-Luc Pepin headed a list of hastily dug-up government witnesses who stoutly defended Ford. Pepin told the committee that Ford, which had then been restructuring its operations, faced difficulties meeting the Canadian value-added requirement for its cars. But, he added, it later went out into Canadian industry and far exceeded the government's requirement by generating an additional $200 million worth of business to compensate for its difficulties. (Out of sheer charity, no doubt.)

"This represents new production over and above the company's promise and includes considerable new employment that would not otherwise have developed," hailed Pepin, who added he had "only praise" for Ford.

Then came Herb Gray's turn and, in Winch's own words, he fairly tripped over himself in rushing to Ford's defence. He amplified what Pepin had said, spoke of the company's "splendid record," pointing out how the two new plants Pepin had spoken of had been built in his own home town of Windsor.

Gray "questioned" government officials, frequently consulting with them privately before, and asked them to "please briefly explain to the committee" the wonderful achievements of the Ford Motor Company.

Committee Chairman Hales himself also found it "odd" that his committee members spent a great deal of time criticizing Auditor-General Maxwell Henderson for blowing the whistle on Ford and the thirteen other companies in his

1967 and 1968 reports—even though Henderson had acted properly, and hadn't even named the companies or amounts.

Gray blustered that Henderson's reports were an "insult to Ford," and attacked him for not investigating further and discovering that the government planned to forget about the duties owed.

Hales noted that Henderson "fulfilled his functions properly" and Winch put it a bit stronger: "When the auditor-general brings in things that they don't like, then they try to run down the man and discredit what he says. It's a disgraceful way to avoid the truth." He dismissed Gray as "nothing but an apologist for Ford."

Winch didn't get too far trying to get a straight answer from witnesses about why Ford's two major competitors—General Motors and Chrysler—had no difficulty meeting the pact's requirements.

Even more importantly, the committee, while it considered Ford's "contributions," should also have reviewed the company's financial position and profits.

But when Winch pointed out to the committee that Ford's profits had jumped from $7,351,000 in 1964—the year before the pact—to $50,200,000 in 1968, Herb Gray and his Liberal Colleagues cried out "Red herring!"

Pepin said that the government hadn't considered Ford's profits in reaching a decision and Hales ordered Winch to stop that line of questioning.

"They just weren't interested," said Winch, "in hearing anything but what was good for Ford. If it's relevant to know what Ford did for the economy, then surely it's relevant to know whether they needed $75 million of the tax-payer's money."

He also casts some doubt on Ford's accomplishments in the last four years, which Gray and the officials heralded as reason enough to forget about the duties.

During the years 1962-65, Ford spent more investment capital and gave more additional employment than it did between 1966 and 1970.

"But again, this was ruled irrelevant. I wonder why."

Winch also wondered why the government, which knew in 1967 that Ford had failed to meet the requirements, waited more than eighteen months before issuing its forgiveness order.

Perhaps Ford's contributions were not so much to the general economy, enough to merit such government understanding, but to the Liberal Party.

"I'd also like to know Ford's campaign contributions," Winch told reporters (but was never quoted in any newspaper). "I'm sure they did contribute, but to whom?"

Winch vainly asked for a commission of enquiry "since the Public Accounts Committee has failed to do its job."

"You don't see the government rushing to forgive an old-age pensioner or a veteran a penny of income tax," he said, "but they rush to bootlick the millionaires and a lot of people wonder why."

Great things should be expected from the new minister in charge of keeping watch on American investment.

Brave Talk
by Robert Chodos

As is not uncommon in Ottawa, most of the action was somewhere else.

But the reverberations were felt there with unusual severity. There is really only one issue in Canadian politics just now and that is jobs, and what was happening in Washington, in particular, meant that there were fewer jobs than there would otherwise be.

The operative word was uncertainty. The government was uncertain where the Americans were heading. It was uncertain what we would do to deal with emerging American protectionism. Its forecasts of unemployment had been wrong, but that was because people were participating in the labour force at a higher rate than usual; it had correctly predicted the number of jobs available. It would predict neither employment nor unemployment for the coming winter. And it was uncertain about the reason for the rise in the participation rate.

Prime Minister Trudeau had some suggestions as to why it might have occurred, however: "It may be because the work ethic is coming back or because women's lib has convinced more women that they should be looking for work because it's the right thing to do or because students are browned off with universities and they want to do their own thing for a while."

In reality, of course, the reasons were not quite so mystical. If students were not going to university in the usual numbers—and they were not—it had more to do with the decline in the economic value of the university degree than with any return of the work ethic. And it had most to do with the difficulty students had last summer in finding jobs (40 per cent of students' educational costs are financed from summer earnings); despite the government's Opportunities for Youth program, unemployment among people under

*Published in the *Last Post*, November 1971.

twenty-five was 10.8 per cent in July and 9.1 per cent in August.

In other words, the rise in the participation rate was directly related to the tightening of the economy. And besides, even if the participation rate had remained the same as last September, the seasonally adjusted unemployment rate would still have been well over 6 per cent.

Clearly, the answers lay elsewhere. Government officials' uncertainty was, no doubt, part of the truth, but it was also good cover for another part: what they did know about Canada's economic prospects was not comforting, and they were plainly scared.

They knew, for instance, that the United States was prepared to be tough in demanding the removal of the clauses in the Canada-US auto pact that protected Canadian jobs. They knew that any Canadian government measure designed to stimulate employment—from the Employment Support Bill to counteract the effects of the Nixon surcharge, to a regional-development grant, to the Michelin tire plant in Nova Scotia—could run into opposition from south of the border. And they knew that, economic relations between the two countries being what they are, the Americans had the clout to get their way.

They knew, finally, that one of their most cherished illusions was precisely that. There was, in the end, no special relationship with the United States.

This is not an aspect of reality that is easy for the Liberal Party to face. For the special relationship was not just something the party had adopted out of convenience, something that could be easily cast aside like the policy of opposition to nuclear weapons. It was, historically, their very raison d'être as a party, the cornerstone of their philosophy, the thing that differentiated them from the Conservatives, who believed in high tariff walls and the British connection.

When he was talking about our range of options at his October 15 press conference, Trudeau observed that the 1911 election had been fought on the issue of reciprocity versus no-truck-or-trade-with-the-Yankees. He recalled wistfully that no-truck-or-trade-with-the-Yankees had won.

But that victory was short-lived. The special relationship soon came back in the form of Mackenzie King and C. D. Howe, who gave the idea economic flesh and bone and made it work. And so Canada got a slightly diluted version of American prosperity, complete with the high standard of living, the forty-hour work week and stereo.

And, the Liberals figured, it could go on forever. There were a few who questioned whether this was, in fact, the best thing we could be doing with this country, but they could be dismissed as revolutionaries, romantics and impractical dreamers.

Until August 15, 1971.

Even after the original Nixon message, the import of what he had said took a while to sink in. This is obviously some sort of mistake, Ottawa said. Surely you don't mean us.

The first sign that Ottawa was getting the message came, appropriately, at the Centre for Inter-American Relations in New York City. There, in a September 21 address, Mitchell Sharp, the mild-mannered secretary of state for External Affairs, said that "the enunciation of the Nixon Doctrine, and more particularly its specific manifestation in the economic measures taken by the United States last month, has effectively, and perhaps brutally, challenged some of our assumptions and led us to re-examine our position as an industrial and trading nation."

In the code-language of diplomacy, he added: "I hesitate to believe that the United States is now turning its back on a partnership in the development that has served both our societies well for centuries." He hesitated to believe it, but he had made the suggestion. Then he said, "I do not accept that the United States, in a narrow and short-sighted pursuit of its own interests, has adopted a beggar-my-neighbour policy towards Canada." Now he had made that suggestion too.

Two days later, Ron Collister of the CBC asked Prime Minister Trudeau on the television program *Encounter:* "The President's measures, do you think they show a fundamental change in US trade policy? Are we going to have to make fundamental changes in ours in reaction?"

"Yes," answered the prime minister.

Later in the program he added that "When the Americans look at what they're doing they say: 'Well you know, we're doing this to the Japanese and we're doing this to the Europeans,' they don't seem to realize what they're doing to Canadians. If they do realize what they're doing and if it becomes apparent that they just want us to be sellers of natural

Robert Chodos / 137

resources to them and buyers of their manufactured products—all these 'ifs'—I repeat we will have to reassess fundamentally our relation with them, trading, political and otherwise."

It was brave talk. Trudeau said that our options ranged all the way from a trade war to a common market with the United States (from no-truck-or-trade to reciprocity), and that was brave talk too.

For it is in the very nature of reciprocity that both parties have to want it for it to come off. And even with Ottawa's inability to gauge American intentions it could perceive that reciprocity was something in which the Americans were not interested.

As for a trade war, if it was to be waged successfully it required firepower and the willingness to use it. Observers noted with interest the government's verbal escalation, which quickly became standard fare in ministerial speeches, and waited to see whether it would be backed up with anything more substantial.

They are still waiting. The American Treasury Department said that it had a shopping list of grievances against Canada and Mitchell Sharp replied that he had a shopping list of grievances against the United States. But, unlike the Americans, he didn't give any indication of what he might do to have his grievances redressed.

One did not envy him his chances of success. The uncertainty of American intentions was genuine, although some possibilities—the ones the Liberal government had devoutly hoped for—had now been eliminated. The exact reason why the Nixon administration leaked the shopping list was unknown; some have suggested that it was meant as an indirect message to the recalcitrant Japanese. Nor was it known why the story was given wildly inordinate prominence by the *Chicago Tribune,* a newspaper so faithful to the administration as to be almost its unofficial spokesman.

Stripped of its fundamental assumptions and unable to see any substitutes it would find palatable, the government gave the impression of proceeding from day to day, reacting to events, moving this way and then that. It had discovered that a Canadian cabinet minister could criticize the United States in public without the sky falling in. And it was evidently eager to pursue its new-found friendship with the Soviet Union.

But a co-ordinated, decisive independent course still seemed far beyond its power.

The Great Canadian DREE Machine
by Robert Chodos

No one believes in Santa Claus any more

A red-black-and-white billboard, in any number of towns in Quebec or the Atlantic provinces, announces that the school, road or sewer system under construction is another project of the Government of Canada, Department of Regional Economic Expansion. A press release, faithfully reproduced in the local paper, says that thanks to $37,400 of the department's money, some enterprising company is going to build a factory in Three Rivers, or Sherbrooke, or Truro, and create jobs for twenty-four people.

The basic message is JOBS.

The public image of Jean Marchand, minister of regional economic expansion, has always been mixed because of his unusual style. As a Quebec labour leader, as a minister in the Pearson cabinet, as one of the most prominent men in the Trudeau government, he has been highly successful in making enemies as well as friends.

But there was no such mixed image of his Department of Regional Economic Expansion (known as DREE) when it was set up in 1969. Its creation fulfilled one of the few pledges Pierre Elliott Trudeau had bothered to make in his 'no promises' election campaign the previous year. After his election sweep, Trudeau asked his long-time friend and principal lieutenant Marchand what portfolio he wanted. Marchand asked for DREE and got it.

The new department was seen everywhere as a sign of hope—especially in Atlantic Canada, where regional underdevelopment is most deeply rooted. There had been despair over the failure of earlier attempts by the federal government to help lagging regions. DREE was to be different. Instead of small, jerry-built programs there was to be an all-out attack on one of the major weaknesses of Cana-

*Published in the Last Post, July 1972.

dian confederation. Ottawa promised regional equality and, not surprisingly, there was little public criticism of the new department for two years, while people waited for the promises to be fulfilled.

Then, in late 1971, the honeymoon came to an end. Where there had been eager waiting, suddenly there was a series of broadsides against the department.

The most widely publicized criticism came from the Atlantic Provinces Economic Council (APEC)—an organization sponsored by the four provincial governments and by private individuals. It devoted its fifth annual review of the Atlantic economy, released last October, entirely to the work of DREE.

APEC does not quarrel with everything. It accepts the idea of a federal department for regional development, and asks for a ten-year guarantee that DREE will get enough money to continue. Further, it accepts the main instrument the department uses in trying to carry out its aims—grants to private corporations.

But, APEC complains, the department's programs are badly planned, subject to political pressure, administered by a bureaucracy that is too centralized and too unresponsive.

It feels that it's "next to impossible" to find out how large a grant has to be to convince a firm to locate in a particular area. It says the advantages that DREE supposedly gives the Atlantic provinces—by allowing maximum grants there to be higher than in other areas—are more apparent than real, since the department rarely gives the maximum grant anyway. It notes that these advantages, such as they were, were further eroded by the decision to make the highly developed Montreal region eligible for DREE grants, as of January 1, 1971. APEC also attacks the government's concentration on infrastructure—developers' jargon for public works—which it says does not directly contribute to regional economies. It suggests that these projects are chosen because they are highly visible and show men and machines at work.

Further, it says that Marchand's wide powers leave his department open to political pressure, maintains that planning for the Atlantic provinces cannot be done effectively from far-away Ottawa and asks for a regional office to carry out all DREE activities for the area.

Heavy criticism from one of the main areas of the country

supposedly being helped by the DREE programs was bad enough, but more was to come. A few weeks after the Atlantic Provinces Economic Council report, a similar document was made public by the Quebec Federation of Labour, whose new political consciousness was just beginning to surface.

Marchand and Trudeau have been particularly sensitive to criticisms of the department that come from Quebec, which is widely regarded as DREE's favoured child. When Premier Robert Bourassa told Trudeau last November that Ottawa's campaign against regional inequality had accomplished little, the prime minister, according to Arthur Blakely of the *Montreal Gazette*, "reacted with shocked disbelief."

The Quebec Federation of Labour report does more than just echo APEC's criticisms. It goes further and attacks the whole concept of the giveaway policy. It says DREE has not changed the structure of the Quebec economy (just as APEC said about the Atlantic economy). It says DREE has perpetuated outside control of Quebec's economy, that it has neglected the poorest parts of the province in favour of those that are economically stronger, and that the new employment it creates is often offset by layoffs or shutdowns elsewhere, sometimes in the same companies that get the grants. Government grants, it says, have eliminated the risk factor from private enterprise—the usual justification for private profit.

The QFL's onslaught against DREE concludes that small and medium-sized companies cannot meet the challenge of regional development, and that for large enterprises, the government grants are gifts, pure and simple.

Attacks on DREE continued to pop up at an increasing rate. Ottawa's own Science Council said that regional incentives were only making inefficient industries even more inefficient. "There is a place for small-scale manufacturing in the less-developed provinces," it said in its report on Canadian manufacturing, "as the success of many companies attests. Manufacturing industry is not, however, the ultimate solution to the development of these areas, since it fails to make use of their inherent advantages."

The next major blow-up came over the Atlantic Development Council's ten-year strategy for the Atlantic region.

The ADC is an advisory group, made up of people in the

Atlantic provinces and responsible to DREE. It had submitted its strategy to Marchand in January 1971. This recommended that the main objectives for the next ten years should be "to achieve adequate employment opportunities for the region's population," to reduce the rate at which people were moving away from the area, and "to bring about structural changes in the economy which will ensure for the future a high and self-sustaining level of activity."

How should this be done? The Atlantic Development Council said the need was to develop manufacturing, and particularly secondary manufacturing; complexes of related industries should be emphasized. Although it said that resource-based industries should also be "systematically explored and promoted," the ADC declared that these would not provide enough jobs by themselves. In fact, as resource-based industries were rationalized, there would be a loss in jobs that would have to be made up elsewhere.

The targets set by the ADC were 170,000 jobs by 1981, with 50,000 of them in the manufacturing sector, and $25 billion in capital investment. It emphasized the importance of these targets as "a guide to public policy," as a "challenge" to "each individual and business organization," and as "a yardstick against which public and private actions can be measured."

The ADC strategy was based on what Atlantic economists had been saying for years. And since the ADC was responsible to DREE, it was regarded with some hope in the region.

Marchand made no comment for almost a year. Then, on January 14 of this year, he told the ADC that he was accepting the plan.

"We wholeheartedly agree," he said, "with the essence of this strategy. Much of what my department has done in its relatively short life has been consistent with it." But he refused to accept the targets set by the council. Too many unknowns, he said... depends on performance of national and international economies... more effective decision-making needed. At a subsequent press conference, he tossed off a disparaging remark about promising jobs, noting Premier Bourassa's ill-fated promise to create 100,000 jobs in Quebec by the end of 1971.

The chairman of the ADC, William Smith, sat next to Marchand, visibly disappointed. He gently chided the minister for not accepting *some* targets, so that there would be some way of knowing if the department's policies had succeeded or failed. The Atlantic Provinces Economic Council followed with another broadside in its monthly newsletter, saying that Marchand's refusal to accept the targets was "as inexplicable as it is disappointing."

"It calls into question once again the federal government's dedication to the long-term development of the Atlantic Provinces on a planned and orderly basis and reinforces the suspicion that DREE is nothing more than a well-financed giveaway program to be extended or contracted according to the economic and political exigencies of the moment."

Marchand continued to take credit for accepting the ADC strategy; his critics continued to attack his department for not accepting the core of that strategy, the targets.

It was back to square one.

Did DREE give up on the East?

A major turning point in the history of DREE occurred on January 1, 1971, when amendments to the map of designated areas went into effect. Added were all previously undesignated parts of Quebec, along with the eastern tip of Ontario. To cushion the effect this would have on the Atlantic provinces, maximum grants for capital costs in the Atlantic region were raised to 35 from 25 per cent (a gain that was largely illusory, since almost all DREE grants are below the maximum).

Before the changes, 38.3 per cent of the money given in grants had gone to firms establishing in the province of Quebec, and 34.1 per cent had gone to the Atlantic provinces. After the changes, Quebec got 54.4 per cent, the Atlantic provinces 17.3.

$34,752,000 in RDIA grants had gone to Quebec up until December 1970; from January 1971 to March 1972, it got $82,637,000. The Atlantic provinces got $30,913,000 up to December 1970, and $26,357,000 from January 1971 to March 1972.

Quebec's share has increased steadily: it got 39.3 per cent in the first six months of 1971, 53.6 per cent in the last six months of that year, and fully 74.8 per cent in the first three months of 1972. Even when one very large grant

($13,770,000 to International Telephone and Telegraph for a paper mill on the North Shore of the St. Lawrence) is discounted, Quebec still got 61.9 per cent in those three months.

These proportions do not in themselves prove discrimination against the Atlantic provinces. But they do raise serious questions about the nature of the incentives program.

Of all the provinces, Quebec comes closest to reproducing in miniature the structure of the Canadian economy as a whole. Parts of it—the Gaspé and Lower St. Lawrence regions—are economically similar to the neighbouring Atlantic provinces. Along with the Atlantic region, eastern Quebec forms the severest challenge for any regional-development policy in Canada.

On the other hand the Montreal area—the bulk of the new area designated in January 1971—is as heavily industrialized as southern Ontario, although incomes in Montreal are lower. People from the outlying regions of Quebec pour into Montreal in search of jobs, just as Maritimers pour into Toronto and people from the prairies into Vancouver.

Not even Jean Marchand ever said that the problems facing Montreal in late 1970 were regional-development problems. Rather, he has maintained it was a short-term unemployment problem caused by a lag in investment in the Montreal area. "If you study the economic evolution of Montreal in relation to Toronto, for example," he told Tory regional-development critic Jim McGrath in the Commons Committee on Regional Development on April 27, 1972, "you see that for many years they were progressing at the same rate and now Montreal is going this way in relation to Toronto. So that is what we have tried to balance out now, and we have been successful."

Even granting Marchand his estimation of his success, and granting him his interpretation of the problem in Montreal (others have suggested that the designation of Montreal and the Quebec Crisis of October 1970 were not unrelated), it is still possible to ask whether DREE was the proper instrument to deal with that problem.

Marchand and department officials have always said that DREE is not an anti-unemployment measure. They have emphasized the importance of looking at the long term. The use of development grants to deal with short-term problems in Montreal is in direct conflict with that, and the impact of the incentives program in the areas for which it was intended could not help but suffer.

The low proportion of grants going to the Atlantic provinces is matched by a low proportion of applications coming from there. From January 1971 to March 1972 there were 407 applications for RDIA grants to set up plants in the Atlantic provinces, or 15.7 per cent of the total across the country. Quebec had 2074 applications—63.3 per cent of the total; of those, 1300 were for the newly named region around Montreal.

One of the difficulties with a policy of grants to private corporations is that it forces the minister to be a 'passive onlooker'. He can only react to applications; he cannot initiate projects. The success or failure of his policy ultimately depends on whether it fits in with what private corporations want to do or, as economist Kari Levitt put it at a regional-planning conference in Winnipeg last autumn, "the only serious planning that is done in Canada is done by large corporations."

So, if corporations want to get their grants in Montreal instead of in Moncton or Corner Brook, there is little the department can do.

The facts are consistent with themselves. Since the designation of Montreal, 21.9 per cent of unemployed people living in designated areas are in the Atlantic provinces. The region has received 18.3 per cent of the grants by number, and 17.3 per cent by value. 15.7 per cent of the applications have come from there. The department has fourteen officers specifically assigned to handling applications from the Atlantic region, as compared to forty-two for Quebec. The only office for processing applications that the department maintains outside Ottawa is in Montreal.

The question is: what ever happened to the original intention of the program to attract industry to the Atlantic region? Has DREE given up on the Atlantic provinces?

Patronage? Conflict of interest?

Other questions are being asked about the incentives program too.

On March 1, John Burton (NDP—Regina East) demanded an emergency debate in the House of Commons on possible conflict of interest in DREE. The charge was based on the membership of the minister's advisory board, which includes several businessmen representing corporations that have received DREE grants.

One member of the board, Kendall Cork, is vice-president and treasurer of Noranda Mines Ltd., which has received a DREE grant of $3,522,000, and whose subsidiary Gaspé Copper Mines Ltd. has received a grant of $3,627,000. Another board member is Jack Estey, executive vice-president of National Sea Products Ltd., which has received three DREE grants totalling $2,229,701. M. W. MacKenzie, retired chairman of the board of Chemcell Ltd., which has received grants totalling $406,923, is also on the advisory board.

In the Regional Development Committee on April 27, Burton pressed the same line of attack. This time he brought up the case of George McClure, who joined DREE on February 24, 1969, and left the department on August 1, 1970, to accept an executive position with McCain Foods Ltd. In the time McClure was with DREE, three grants totalling $7.1 million were made to McCain Foods.

The department replies that the advisory board is an advisory body only and makes no final decisions. Furthermore, its meetings are confidential so that we cannot know whether it discussed the grants in question, although Deputy Minister Doug Love told the committee the board had never discussed the Gaspé Copper grant. As for McClure, Love said he was not in the incentives division but in operations east, which does not handle incentives, and an investigation had "failed to reveal any evidence that would give rise to legitimate concern about conflict of interest."

Wally Lavigne, assistant deputy minister for incentives, dismisses the suggestion that RDIA grants are used for patronage purposes of any kind with a contemptuous "horseshit!"

But patronage and conflict of interest are matters of definition. Canadian Johns-Manville, Falconbridge Nickel, IBM, Union Carbide, Westinghouse and the Steel Company of Canada were among the corporations represented at a major Liberal Party $50-a-plate fund-raising dinner in Toronto March 1. All have received DREE grants, ranging from

$126,000 for Stelco to $6 million for IBM. Is that patronage? Or merely a perfectly normal coincidence?

Of course, corporations identified with the Conservative Party have also received DREE grants, including Stanfield's Ltd., the opposition leader's family's underwear business in Truro. And the proposition that DREE has gone out of its way to favour specifically Liberal corporations would be impossible to prove.

Perhaps the real point is not that there is conflict of interest between working for DREE and then going to work for McCain's, but rather that there is no conflict of interest—the interests are the same.

Another charge that has been levelled against the department is that it often doesn't create jobs, but at best moves them from one place to another. The Quebec Federation of Labour, in its report on DREE, cites several cases of recipients of DREE grants that had laid off workers—for example Bruck Mills Ltd., which received $843,105 to create 140 jobs at its textile mills in Sherbrooke and Cowansville, Quebec, and laid off ninety-five workers at the Sherbrooke mill, or Swecan Saw, which received $129,486 to create forty-eight jobs at its plant in Lanorie d'Autray and laid off nineteen workers at the same plant.

The $13-million-plus grant to ITT for a pulp-and-paper complex on the North Shore, coming at a time when Canadian International Paper was closing a paper mill at Temiscaming in northwestern Quebec, throwing several hundred workers out of their jobs, was widely criticized. And so were grants to firms that closed down their southern Ontario operations to move into designated areas. Union Carbide received $1.3 million to move from Welland, Ont., to Beauharnois, Quebec, while Aerovox Canada received $235,000 to move from Hamilton to Amherst, NS.

For these, too, the department has its reasons. The ITT complex and the CIP mill have nothing to do with each other, say departmental officials; besides, the pulp-and-paper industry has to be rationalized and the closing of the obsolete, inefficient Temiscaming mill accompanied by the construction of the modern, efficient ITT complex is an important step in that direction.

The companies that were subsidized to move from Ontario elsewhere often would have closed their Ontario operations anyway, according to the department. It was a question of getting them to establish somewhere in Canada or having them leave the country. Competition for foreign investment is keen, and other countries offer much more generous concessions than Canada. If we want to get our slice of the pie, we have to know how to play the game.

Or else we should be questioning whether we want to be in the game at all.

"The situation has really not changed"

"IBM needs a grant from the Canadian taxpayer," Kari Levitt told the Winnipeg planning conference, "like I don't know who needs what. The situation has certainly become quite, quite absurd."

The rationale for giving grants to small entrepreneurs, who are often blocked from starting new enterprises by a shortage of capital, is clear enough. But as the QFL pointed out, the challenge of regional development cannot be met by small enterprises.

What is the justification for giving grants to corporations like IBM, Michelin Tire, ITT, Westinghouse and Procter & Gamble, which are not short of capital by any stretch of the imagination?

Let Jean Marchand explain:

"It's not a present that I'm giving. Because an enterprise, for example IBM, would prefer to be in Metropolitan Toronto or elsewhere, so I tell it: if you come establish yourself in Granby, I will compensate you for the economic disadvantages that that implies for the company; I won't give you a present; I will simply compensate you for the economic disadvantages."

Marchand has been consistent in citing this rationale for incentive grants. However, the grants are calculated not on the basis of economic disadvantage but on the basis of capital costs and jobs created. Economist Roy George of the University of Toronto has shown that in strict dollars-and-cents terms, there is *no* economic disadvantage to establishing a manufacturing plant in Nova Scotia rather than in Ontario: the higher cost of transportation is made up by lower labour costs. George attributes the absence of industry in Nova Scotia to lack of entrepreneurship; according to Kari Levitt, there are many factors at work—for example, any manufacturer making a product that requires servicing will want to be close to where the product has to be serviced.

Wally Lavigne has said, "The grants are incentives: they are to incite firms to establish in a designated area," and this is perhaps closer to what they are all about. The government says in effect, "If you don't want to go into a designated area, there's nothing we can do. If you do, we'll sweeten things a little by giving you some money." The corporation says, "Okay, if you give us two million we'll go. Now let's work that out in terms of numbers of jobs created and percentage of capital costs."

One suggestion often made is that the government should buy equity in the companies it finances, instead of just giving them money; that it should keep some ownership and control. The NDP has repeatedly advanced the suggestion; Tory critic Jim McGrath sees some merit in it; privately, even some DREE officials agree.

"Under the Incentives Act, if the act is well implemented," Marchand told Arnold Peters (NDP—Timiskaming) in the regional-development committee, "I do not think we are justified in asking for that. If you want to invest in northern Ontario, you need a grant because you will be at a disadvantage in relation to your competitors, so you say, 'If you want me to go there, I need a grant of $1 million; otherwise I will not be on an equal footing and I will not be able to compete.'

"If we think it is in the public interest to have your plant there, all we do is compensate you for a disadvantage that we impose on you in the name of the public interest. Why should we ask for shares? What would be the moral justification? You would say, 'All right. Keep your $1 million and I will go elsewhere and be in a position to compete without your $1 million.'"

"Except," replied Peters, "that the people should be protected in being able to say, 'You damn well do not operate with our resource unless you do this,' and putting money in it should give us some equity in it."

One might well ask Marchand what the moral justification is in giving $6 million to IBM.

In fact, the department is beginning to experiment with buying equity through its Newfoundland Development Corporation, just getting underway. In another experiment, its New Brunswick Multiplex Corporation is trying to attract a group of related industries to Saint John. Neither of these programs has been in existence long enough to be evaluated, but they appear to be signs that the department is having a few healthy doubts of its own about the crude giveaway approach to regional development.

Another oft-heard suggestion is that the government should set up its own enterprises, that it should plan seriously, identify opportunities for industrial development and go into them itself. Public ownership should be a major government instrument for economic growth instead of the last-resort measure to save doomed enterprises that it has tended to be in this country.

"That is something different," Marchand told Peters. "There I would agree much more with you. Should we do more of this—to have a public corporation of our own instead of granting this $1 million? There I would feel much more in agreement with you."

There is no sign that the minister's noble sentiments are about to become department policy.

Marchand says again and again that the gap between unemployment in the Atlantic provinces and unemployment in the country as a whole is closing, but the evidence is at best uncertain. In January 1969, just before DREE came into being, the difference was 4.2 per cent; in January 1970 it was 3.9 per cent; in January 1971 it had been reduced to 2.2 per cent (mostly as a result of an *increase* in unemployment in the rest of the country); and in January 1972 it was back up to 5.2 per cent. There were 493,000 more Canadians employed in January 1972 than there were in January 1969, but only 12,000 of those new jobs were in the Atlantic provinces.

"The situation has really not changed," Kari Levitt said in Winnipeg. "It has only become more absurd because there is a proliferation of both federal and provincial incentives. In this complete zero sum game, the only people who really benefit are the few scamps who operate in this administrative jungle and a number of large firms, or the shareholders of same, who locate in certain areas."

One effect of DREE may be to dispel a long-standing Canadian myth.

There has been a pronounced tendency among social democrats and left-liberals in Canada to equate greater centralization with progress. Provincial governments are regarded as inherently backward and reactionary; the only hope for change lies in Ottawa. The Regina Manifesto is as centralist a document as has ever been produced in this country, and CCFers and New Democrats have remained faithful to that aspect of their original statement of principles, if not to others. It is only recently that some radicals, particularly in Quebec, have fought to take powers away from Ottawa rather than give more powers to it.

But in this army of centralizers one prominent Canadian political theorist always stood out as a dissenter.

"The first task of the socialist," wrote Pierre Elliott Trudeau in 1961, "is to educate all of the people to demand maximum service from all of their governments ... Most of the reforms that could come about through greater centralization could also follow from patient and painstaking cooperation between federal and provincial governments. And the remaining balance of economic advantage that might arise from forcefully transferring more power to the central government is easily offset by the political disadvantages of living under a paternalistic or bullying government."

The Economic Domination of Canada
by Pierre Elliott Trudeau

In the summer of 1972, the Trudeau government finally announced its policy on foreign ownership of Canadian industry. After months of nation-wide debate, of battles over the Gray report, of leaks within leaks, this was it: the cabinet would review certain foreign takeovers and step in if they weren't in the national interest. The mildness of the move stunned even the business press.

Since Trudeau was one of the editors of the intellectual journal Cité Libre in the fifties, his many articles on Quebec have been picked clean by the press. But somehow, until the Last Post published these excerpts in the spring of 1972, the essay from which they were taken escaped everyone's attention.

The piece demonstrates, first, that Trudeau foresaw the impending crisis over US investment in Canada long before some of the current nationalist spokesmen. He was no stranger to the issue of economic domination; in fact, he raised it at a time when few people were paying attention to it. Second, the article shows a clear understanding of the mechanics of such domination, and of the political consequences. Trudeau argues for honestly outlining the alternatives to a situation of dependence to the Canadian people, and for vigorous intervention in the economy.

His proposed solutions are set out vaguely, and seem to be a combination of social-democratic economic intervention combined with pressure on Canadian capital to enter the speculative sector more aggressively. It is not fair to imply that the prime minister has turned his back on a socialist past.

But it is fair to wonder if this is the same man who brought down the foreign-ownership policy of the summer of 1972.

*Extracts from an essay in Cité Libre, May 1958, reprinted in the Last Post, May 1972.

In the key sectors of the Canadian economy, non-residents are in a position to take decisions contrary to the well-being of Canadians. And that has in fact come about in industries as important as automobiles, optical products, titanium, radios, chemical products and many others. Foreigners will decide if our oil wells are to be worked or closed, if our ore is to be transformed here or elsewhere, if our factories are to be automated or not, if our products are to be put on the world market or not, or if our workers are to be free to exercise their right of association or not. Foreigners will decide . . . and will collect the profits: in the post-war years, for example, 55 per cent of the dividends paid by the sum total of Canadian companies were distributed to non-residents; at the same time, these people automatically became owners of two-fifths of the accumulated and undistributed profits, strengthening their hold on our economy all the more.

This leads us to the following question: can Canada free herself from the domination exercised by foreigners, particularly Americans, on our economy? . . .

The relative slowing down of the American economy, currently characterized by an unemployment crisis, has in no way allowed Canada to take an advance over its "impoverished" neighbour; far from winning markets at the expense of our neighbours, our own economy has been rendered decrepit as a result of their sickness, as currently witnessed by unemployment here. The reason for it is obvious: not only is the United States our main furnisher of capital, but it also constitutes our principal buyer, having bought, in 1955 for example, 60 per cent of all our exports. Consequently, an American crisis constricts a good part of our investments and of our outlets at the same time . . .

Apart from the exclusion, pure and simple, of American capital, a perfectly reactionary solution which would assume a vigorous braking of our economic expansion and a radical reduction of our standard of living, two attitudes remain possible: Either we shall passively suffer our situation of economic domination, and then it would be better to be annexed outright to the United States, rather than be a colony exploited without limit. Or else we shall intervene vigorously in the game of economic forces by adopting economic policies which take account of the following factors:

The gradual exhaustion of American resources, as stated by the Paley report.

The monopoly held in Canada on certain resources.

The pressing need that the Americans have of finding markets for their surpluses of production and capital.

The existence of such markets in Canada, which unite conditions of economic profitability and political security with rare good fortune.

These facts give Canada a bargaining power which would allow her to direct capital according to the following priorities:

Social profitability must take precedence over economic profitability: houses, schools and hospitals must come before factories and mills . . .

The resources which cannot be preserved, before those which can wait until we need them without dwindling; for example, waterfalls and forests before oil and mines. . .

Finally, instead of harming the development of trade unionism, our governments ought to encourage it. For in the end, when all the capital transactions have been concluded, when the government has obtained the best possible price for natural resources, the workers' unions can still do something: by obtaining maximum salaries for our workers, they leave minimum surpluses abroad.

One may doubtless object here that in negotiating too toughly, Canada may sometimes succeed in banishing foreign capital. Obviously, any agreement between equals is negotiated at this risk, and the parties must read just their conditions and their demands according to their successes and failures.—I add only this: it would not always be a misfortune if we turned foreign capital away from time to time towards countries less demanding and less fortunate than ours. We might thus contribute (where the automatic functioning of capitalist laws is so unsuccessful) to the eventual setting up of the 'civitas maxima', where the good of the international community will have priority over the good of a national state . . .

Canada will not automatically get out of its situation of

economic domination. To get out, it first has to want to.
Now it is not at all certain that Canadians really want to,
since the politicians have never exposed the alternatives to
them. Hence nobody really knows if the Canadian people
would be ready to slow down the rhythm of their progress
slightly, in case it were necessary to conquer a relative
economic independence.

Contributors

Nick Auf der Maur is a founding editor of the *Last Post*, and currently works with the CBC in Montreal.

Robert Chodos is a founding editor of the *Last Post*, and author of the book *Right of Way* on railroad policy.

Gordon Cleveland is a graduate in economics from Carleton University, and worked in the Department of Industry, Trade and Commerce.

Richard Liskeard is a freelance writer in Toronto.

Jim Littleton has been active in the Waffle since 1969, and works as a research consultant at the Ontario Institute for Studies in Education in Toronto.

Rae Murphy is on the editorial board of the *Last Post*.

Mark Starowicz is a founding editor of the *Last Post* and works with the CBC in Toronto.

Ralph Surette is a reporter at the *Montreal Star* specializing in agricultural policy.

Pierre Elliott Trudeau some time ago assumed the post of prime minister, and now lives with his wife and infant son in Ottawa.

John Zaritsky worked in the Ottawa bureau of the *Toronto Star* and is currently with the *Globe and Mail*.

Another Last Post Special . . .

Quebec: A Chronicle 1968-1972

This book draws together information gathered
on the spot about the most crucial events of
the last four years in Quebec — from the first
stirrings of rebellion in the industrial towns,
in the Mouvement du Taxi and among the
'Lapalme guys', to the drama of the October
crisis. It goes on to describe the birth of the
labour unions' Common Front in the La Presse
strike and, in an important final chapter, ana-
lyzes the Front's spectacular show of strength
in May 1972.

Edited by Last Post staffers Robert Chodos
and Nick Auf der Maur, *Quebec: A Chronicle*
is based on articles which were first published
in the pages of the Last Post.

Paper only $1.95